HAUNTED
RACINE

RORY GRAVES

Published by Haunted America
A Division of The History Press
Charleston, SC
www.historypress.com

First published 2023

Manufactured in the United States

ISBN 9781467150781

Library of Congress Control Number: 2023937203

Notice: The information in this book is true and complete to the best of our knowledge. It is offered without guarantee on the part of the author or The History Press. The author and The History Press disclaim all liability in connection with the use of this book.

An 1883 illustration of the city of Racine. *Property of Racine Heritage Museum, All Rights Reserved.*

Instead of, or perhaps in addition to the supernatural, old buildings are haunted by their memories: memories of those who once inhabited them, and the memories we bring to them....A haunted house is a memory palace made real: a physical space that retains memories that might otherwise be forgotten or that might remain only in fragments.

—*Colin Dickey,*
Ghostland: An American History in Haunted Places, *2016*

CONTENTS

ACKNOWLEDGEMENTS

During the writing of this book, I felt as though I encountered just about every life event imaginable that would delay my progress. I moved, encountered a pandemic, started a new job, got married, caught COVID-19, went to physical therapy twice, moved again and started another job, among so many other crazy things! Without the help and support of those around me, I don't think I could have ever finished this book or even got to a place in my life where the writing of this book would be possible. With that being said, I would like to extend special thanks to just some of the wonderful people who helped me get where I am today.

To Hollace Graves, my wife, who helped me stay on track and became my assistant extraordinaire while researching, interviewing for and writing this book.

To Dr. David Bruce, my former history professor, who inspired me to pursue my passion of writing history and always believed in me, even when I did not believe in myself.

To the Racine Heritage Museum and most especially the head archivist, Mary Nelson, for shaping me into the person I am today, teaching me so much about my community, city and county and providing so much of the research material and photographs that went into this project.

To Amy Dahlquist, who helped me with site research and was always on call for my numerous title, deed and property–related questions.

And to all those I interviewed for this book—thank you so much. Without your stories, I wouldn't have a book at all. Thank you for allowing this novice author to share your experiences through my book. I hope it might shed some light on the truly rich and storied history of this county and the bizarre and unwritten history of Racine's paranormal presences.

AUTHOR'S NOTE

P lease be aware that many of the locations contained in this book are private properties and residences. As such, the author urges readers against trespassing on any of said properties and to respect these places' and people's privacy. Thank you for reading!

PART I

HAUNTED DOWNTOWN

Downtown Racine, Wisconsin, prides itself on being an "artsy, historic, lakefront town," according to the city's official webpage on the district. Since the founding of Racine in 1848, everyone, it seems, wanted to be downtown—on the lake and near the action. Due to its location on both Lake Michigan and against the mouth of the Root River, the area was ideal for both travel and industry, making it a popular port that, in its heyday, rivaled even Milwaukee and Chicago.

Today, downtown Racine has survived through years of change, some negative and some positive, but still, it remains the heart of the city as a community. As one passes down Main Street and the side streets that make up the district, rows of historic buildings mixed in with the occasional modern façade are visible. Each building houses small businesses, restaurants, apartments, bars and other community gathering places. Year round, events like the city's Fourth of July festival (Fourth Fest) and fall celebration (Party on the Pavement) draw people to downtown Racine time and time again. With all the history and energy that live in downtown, it is no wonder that the area is also home to several reportedly haunted locations.

Chapter 1

The Blake Opera House and the Old Stone Building

At the corner of Sixth Street and College Avenue, near the heart of Racine's downtown area, stands an ornate Queen Anne building. Constructed with Cream City bricks and terra cotta, it has red sandstone trim, pressed tin embellishments and beautiful bay windows with tin sunburst motifs. It overlooks the historic Sixth Street district of downtown Racine. The building was erected there in 1886 by the renowned area architect James Gilbert Chandler (1856–1924) and has since become an icon of the downtown area. This building, however, was not the first icon to sit on this lot. In 1882, four years before the building was constructed, one of the most exquisite buildings ever built in the city of Racine stood on the very same spot—at least until one chilly December evening when disaster struck.

The Blake Opera House Fire

In the late 1800s, Racine was both the "Belle City of the Lake" and an important industrial hub of Wisconsin, home to dozens of businesses known both nationally and internationally. This economic boom brought the city a great deal of wealth and fame, and prominent citizens at the top of the economic chain used their influence to build many of the notable Racine landmarks that still exist in the city. One of these wealthy elites was a man

The Blake Opera House, exterior. *Property of Racine Heritage Museum, All Rights Reserved.*

by the name of Lucius S. Blake (1816–1894). A friend to the arts, Blake desperately wanted Racine to have its very own opera house. With a little campaigning, the man brought together several of the city's wealthiest entrepreneurs, including Jerome I. Case (1819–1991), Charles S. Beebe (1843–1936) and John T. Fish (1834–1900), and funded a project to create the Blake Opera House. James M. Wood (1841–1923), a Chicago architect who was well known for his theater designs, quickly got to work.

The Blake Opera House was opened in December 1882 to rave reviews. The *Racine Advocate* declared that it was a "marvel of beauty," and the *Racine Daily Journal* waxed that it was "a palatial opera house that cannot be excelled in the west." The architect, Wood, was so proud of his work that he even stayed on to become the opera house's first manager. The building stood six stories high and housed not only the opera house but also several stores and a fine hotel. The Blake was the pride of Racine, and every newspaper in the area fawned over each ornate detail. The main theater was built to accommodate 1,250 people and housed a beautiful sixty-five-foot-wide stage flanked by two pagodas that had tall painted and gilded turned wooden columns. The pagodas contained private boxes that were, according to the *Racine Advocate*, "draped with the most costly fabrics, the materials being a combination of silk turcoman in crushed strawberry, old blue embossed silk plush and bands of jute valeur, looped back with a magnificent loop and tassels."

The top of the stage was framed with a proscenium arch, above which was a splendid and ornate fresco of Orpheus, the Greek demigod of song, leading his wife from Hades back to the world again. The curtains below were created exclusively for the Blake and used rich strawberry, blue and gold hues.

The walls of the theater were covered in "an elegant design of terra cotta on gold ground," according to the *Advocate*, and the floors had rich and plush carpeting from Brussels. The opulence of the theater was only furthered by the ceiling, across which a huge mural was painted with vines and trellises covered in blooming flowers over a blue sky with cheerful swallows flying overhead. In the middle hung a grand chandelier made of polished brass, porcelain candles and "graceful festoons of crystal, which reflect their prismatic lights spreading a charming effect," as reported by the *Advocate*. The light fixtures in the theater were ornate gas lamps, designed to match the main chandelier. The chandelier and the stage lights, however, were lit by incandescent electric lights—one of the first theaters in the United States to do so.

The opening of the beautiful opera house on the evening of December 15, 1882, was attended by over one thousand individuals, each of whom had bought their tickets via an auction hosted a week before. U.S. District Court judge Charles E. Dyer (1834–1905) presented the Blake Opera House as a wonderful Christmas present to the people of Racine, and District Attorney Henry Allen Cooper (1850–1931) accepted the gracious gift on behalf of the citizens, declaring, "Surely this temple of drama must prove a perpetual source of enjoyment for the people of Racine." Bach's Orchestra of Milwaukee played music during the opening ceremony, and a performance of "Esmeralda" by New York's Madison Square Theater Company followed.

Only two short years later, disaster would strike. On the frigid evening of December 28, 1884, the Blake Opera House and its adjoining hotel were still bustling with people, long after the evening's performance of *The Beggar Student*, by New York's Thompson Opera Company, had concluded. The Sunday evening activity was disrupted shortly after midnight when two explosions rocked the building. Flames began to eat away at the ornamental façade of the building and soon the adjoining hotel as well. Hundreds of guests poured out of the building in a panic, some in nothing but their nightclothes in the cold winter air. Yet the first alarm was not sounded until 1:05 a.m., when a police officer doing his nightly rounds spotted the smoke and flames from his post at the intersection of Main and Fifth Streets. Six fire steamers, including the L.S. Blake, named after the opera house's own

The Blake Opera House, interior. *Property of Racine Heritage Museum, All Rights Reserved.*

benefactor, arrived ten minutes later, but by that time, the fire had already engulfed the entire northeast end of the building. Efforts by the volunteer fire brigade hastily shifted from putting out the fire to preventing the spread of the blaze as the December evening winds continued to feed the spread of the inferno.

The servants' quarters were located in the upper stories of the hotel; they were the first to be cut off from the rest of the building when the rafters came crashing down, blocking the exits. Hundreds of residents of Racine were now out on the street, watching as the firefighters battled the blaze that threatened to swallow the opera house whole. Spectators watched in horror as a woman waved her hands, hanging out of a window on the fourth story, pleading for help. A man below shouted, "Jump for your life!" but before his advice could be heeded, another explosion of flames engulfed the woman and the fourth story. Less than twenty minutes after the fire brigade's arrival, the structure was in ruins. Astoundingly, almost everyone in the building made it out alive. Unfortunately, the fire had claimed the lives of three unfortunate victims. Russell Glover (1839–1884) and his wife, Jennie (unknown–1884), an acting team staying at the hotel, were found amid the ruins several days later, their charred remains still clutching each other. The body of Mrs. S.A. Patrick (unknown–1884), a member of the hotel's housekeeping staff, was never found.

Along with the loss of life came the financial damages. The Thompson Opera Company reported that it lost over $6,000 in assets (about $180,000 in 2023), and the Blake Opera House estimated the fire had done around $197,000 of destruction—an amount worth over $5 million today. The insurance money was paid out and swiftly divvied up between the Blake's stockholders. For the survivors of the fire, multiple benefits were hosted, and money was raised to help them recover. The Blake, however, never did. The opera house was a complete loss, and the building's lot was cleared and sold to the local YMCA.

THE OLD STONE BUILDING

In 1886, the Racine YMCA completed the building that currently stands at 318–24 Sixth Street. The building was to be a state-of-the-art facility with shop spaces on the first floor; offices, clubrooms, reading rooms and a gym on the second floor; sleeping rooms on the third floor; and a bowling alley, swimming pool and bathrooms in the basement. It was a popular destination for many Racinians, so much so that by 1916, the organization had completely outgrown the building and needed a new space. They sold the building to the Knights of Pythias, a fraternal society, which, according to the *Shoreline Leader*, "used the building for their shrouded mysteries for

The Old Stone Building, circa 1900s, exterior. *Property of Racine Heritage Museum, All Rights Reserved.*

34 years." The Pythians rented out the lower-level shop spaces to many different businesses over the years, including the Red Cross Drug Company, then owned by T.W. Thiesen (1867–1925) and George Gates (1871–1958). The drugstore thrived at the location, and by the 1950s, Gates was able to purchase the entire building from the fraternal organization.

The Red Cross Drug Company remained in the building for over seventy years and remained in the Gates family for three generations until a new investor, Emily Hill of Hill & Hill Enterprises, bought the building in 1988 with hopes of restoring it and turning it into apartments, offices, a restaurant and retail space. Though her project was never fully completed, Hill did everything within her power to maintain the integrity of the historic building, which by then had been named as a local landmark by the Racine Landmarks Preservation Commission in 1977. The commission described the building as having many "contrasts of texture and colors…comes closer to the Queen Anne as it was imported to America than do most Queen Anne residences in the city."

The expensive maintenance paid off when Hill was able to sell the building to a couple who had dreams of restoring and transforming the space as well. In 2016, Andy Meyer and Chris Hefel purchased the building from Hill for $279,500. At the time of their purchase, only two of the five storefronts were occupied—one by the Racine Arts Council and the other by the Sixth Street Theatre and Over Our Head Players. The couple put a lot of work into turning the upper floors of the building into the apartment and office spaces they saw, and soon the businesses came to fill the vacant storefronts as well. Currently, the storefronts are occupied by Social on Sixth, an event space; Roberta, a gourmet restaurant; Longshot Vinyl, a record shop and bar; Perennial Handmade Studio, a soap-making shop; and the Sixth Street Theatre. The business owners whose shops reside in the Old Stone Building can agree that there is something off about the building— something perhaps paranormal. Joan Roehre, the owner of Social on Sixth, had many experiences to share.

SOCIAL SPIRITS

Joan Roehre grew up in Racine, and since fifth grade, she has wanted to be a paranormal psychologist. She loved the thrill of being frightened, although she admitted that she isn't often very afraid during her paranormal encounters, of which she has had many. For several years, Roehre was part of the Wisconsin Paranormal Research Society (WPRS), based out of Oconomowoc. She explained that most of the experiences she has had were not that of malevolent spirits but of positive or neutral presences. Roehre joked that the centipedes in the basements often scared her more than the ghosts. Though she loved being part of WPRS investigations, she explained how much work goes into each one, from the hours spent listening to audio recordings to the hours spent sifting through photos just hoping to catch a glimpse of something abnormal. Ultimately, Roehre realized she didn't have enough hours in the day for all the things she wanted to do. Although she left WPRS, Roehre didn't leave the spirits behind.

Nineteen years ago, Roehre joined the Over Our Head Players and has been an active volunteer ever since. The Over Our Head Players base their operations inside a portion of the Old Stone Building, where they have a theater. Upon joining, she did what any good paranormal investigator would do and asked everyone she knew if the place was haunted. The answers were resoundingly "yes" accompanied by an explanation of how they often would hear talking and whispering around the building that couldn't be accounted for. Many refused to even go into the basement of the old building. It wasn't until many years later that Roehre had her first notable experience in the building.

Roehre's first experience occurred one evening when she was in the basement of the building, looking for something. As she was walking back up the stairs, she heard what sounded like hundreds of breaking windows. She felt a gust of wind so strong that it parted her hair and hit the back of her neck. A fellow actor rushed over to ask what the sound had been, but neither of them ever found any explanation.

She thought back to the building's history and the tragic opera house fire that had occurred that chilly and gusty night of December so long ago. Perhaps the sounds were a sort of echo of the event; the sounds of glass shattering could have been the sound of the windows of the opera house breaking from the heat of the fire, and the strong wind could have been the backdraft that often follows such a phenomenon. The more she thought about the event, the more sense it made. Roehre believes the haunting isn't that spirits need help to move on or are stuck in this space in limbo but that it is the energy of these people and events of the past that stick to the building. Both shocks and traumas to a location, like the opera house fire, can be especially powerful. The residual energy causes the disturbances we may interpret as unexplained paranormal activities.

Roehre's involvement with the building wasn't just limited to the theater, either. When Longshot Vinyl opened in 2018, Roehre was attracted to the bar and record shop immediately, calling it her very own Cheers. She became a regular at the business and even hosted several events and fundraisers at the location. She dreamed of having her very own event space like Longshot and soon had her opportunity. When Longshot moved into another storefront within the building, the owner of the building, Chris Hefel, approached Roehre with an offer—an opportunity to lease the old vinyl shop and turn it into the event space she'd dreamed of. Social on Sixth was soon born and became the place to be, hosting a variety of events from brunches to circus performances with all vintage and repurposed items adorning the space.

While preparing the Social on Sixth for a photo shoot, Roehre set up two thirty-foot tables and some chairs before she left for the night. She lined each chair up with the edge of the tiles on the ground, ensuring each was even before leaving for the night. The following morning, she returned to the venue and found the last four chairs on one side of the table were moved out from the table. She asked Andy, who has a workshop in the basement of the building, if he had come upstairs and moved the chairs at any point. Andy said he hadn't in fact moved any of the chairs and that even in the event that he accidentally bumped them, he would have bumped one, not all four of the chairs. Roehre replaced the chairs and didn't think much of it until the following day, when she returned to find the chairs out of place in the exact same way as before. Again, Roehre moved the chairs back, but the next day the chairs were moved into the strange position yet again. The business owner was stumped.

At one point, a good friend of Roehre, who was a pastor, visited the building. Her friend had no prior knowledge on the history of the place. The pastor walked into the back hallway near where the displaced chairs had been and immediately sensed something was off in the space. "There's something in this hallway," she told Roehre. Roehre said that her friend was not the first nor the last to comment on the hallway's odd atmosphere.

Jada Pfarr, the owner of Longshot Vinyl, also admitted that there is something strange about the back hall. When Longshot was still located in the shop space at 324 Sixth Street, now Social on Sixth, she had an eerie experience. Late one slow autumn night, Pfarr and a friend were chatting to pass the time and found themselves on the topic of the ghost that had been turning on the hood light in the kitchen of Roberta. Pfarr joked that she should probably go to check that the light was still off but didn't want to venture through the dark hall that connected the two businesses alone. Her friend volunteered to walk with her, and they entered the dark restaurant, giggling about the silliness of it all. Somewhat relieved, the two found the hood light was still off and returned to Longshot to close up. Pfarr's friend left shortly after.

After she was just about done closing down for the night, Pfarr went back to the shared hallway to check the bathrooms one more time and make sure all the lights were off. Finding everything satisfactory, Pfarr began to walk back down the dark hall to Longshot but started to feel a growing sense of dread and fear well up from within her. She wasn't sure why she suddenly felt so spooked, but she quickly walked back to her business and shut the door behind her, locking it. She was sure she had just been a little on edge from the talk of ghosts earlier in the night and shook the feeling off. As she grabbed her things off the bar and glanced back at the window that looked into the corridor, she froze. A dark shadow passed by where she had been just moments earlier. Pfarr rushed to grab the rest of her things and lock up the business for the night. Though she admitted that she is usually a skeptic when it comes to strange occurrences, she couldn't explain or rationalize what happened to her that night.

"I am not usually a person who spooks easily or has experienced anything supernatural before. I'm not really sure what I experienced that night, and I have tried to reconcile what I saw and felt with my usually practical mind, but it just was a sensation I had never had before and haven't had since. Nor do I want to experience that again!" said Pfarr.

A reporter with the *Racine County Eye*, who also happened to be a medium, once visited Roehre at Social on Sixth. The reporter had no extensive knowledge of the building's rich history. She was there to do a feature on the upcoming 135th anniversary séance. The reporter froze as she entered the building and looked to Roehre. "There's a lot going on here," she said. After descending the stairs into the basement, she felt a deep sadness overcome her senses. She could hear in her head the soft echo of a woman crying out, "My babies! My babies!"

Roehre was struck by the reporter's words and proposed a theory— Jennie Glover, the actress who had died in the fire, was a loving mother to several children. She thought the cries could have been some of Jennie's last laments at leaving them behind. The electromagnetic meter Roehre was holding spiked as she suggested the connection. The two decided to move on to the boiler room, lovingly nicknamed the "murder room" by fellow thespians. When Roehre opened the door, the reporter said she felt as if she'd been stabbed in the chest. The rest of the evening passed uneventfully, but four months later, Roehre received a phone call from the reporter. She claimed that whatever had been with her that night in the boiler room had followed her back home. She still felt uneasy and sought spiritual help from the medium who, by then, had conducted the anniversary séance. Since the phone call, Roehre has not heard back from the reporter.

The medium who conducted the anniversary séance on December 28, 2019, made a lasting impression on Roehre that night. As they began the séance, the medium felt a presence trying to come through. She described a very bold and theatrical masculine energy—the name Russell came to her mind. Roehre was impressed and brought up Russell Glover. The medium agreed that it was certainly possible that it could be the deceased actor. The medium also could smell kerosene and said she had a feeling the opera house fire might not have been an accident. Roehre had heard that the medium she was working with that night was known to be quite accurate and rarely incorrect in her readings. During the séance, the medium heard Roehre's mother coming through. Her mother said she was proud of her and added, "Yes, you are my favorite." Roehre couldn't believe what she was hearing. Those words took her back to the last words she had shared with her mother as she was dying: "Don't forget, I'm your favorite."

Séances aren't the only time the strange history of the Old Stone Building appears, as the Racine Paranormal Investigators (RPI) have also conducted their own investigation on the site. Ron Helmick, the founder of RPI, came with his team and a *Journal Times* reporter to listen to the history of the building. The team's medium, Michael Sorenson, left the building while they discussed the fire to make sure his thoughts would be uninfluenced by the background knowledge. When they finished, Sorenson returned, and with the reporter in tow, he and Roehre did a walkthrough of the building. As they began their tour and entered the back hall, Sorenson immediately saw a congregation of spirits at the end of the hall and joked that it felt like they had a welcoming committee waiting for them. He saw a tall man with a bowler cap flamboyantly motioning for them to come farther. Sorenson was not threatened by the presence and reassured Roehre that they were friendly.

He also sensed the presence of a mischievous spirit near the kitchen and bathroom of Roberta. He asked if anyone ever experienced lights turning on and off, doorknobs turning or randomly locking doors. Roehre confirmed that activity like this was common near the back of the building. She even took her phone with her any time she went to the restroom, citing a foreboding feeling that she would get locked in the bathroom when she was in there. Sorenson told her he could see a male spirit crouching in the corner, chuckling. The spirit was a trickster and was also responsible for moving around items and turning the hood light on and off in Roberta's kitchen from time to time.

Sorenson continued to walk through the building with RPI and Roehre, but he sensed that there was something unique about the building. He felt many different presences, all coming and going from the space. Roehre said he likened it to a paranormal superhighway or a spirit-filled Grand Central Station. There was so much activity packed into this one building, and nowhere was that more apparent than in the basement of the Old Stone Building. Sorenson could see a man, a great influencer in the city, leaning over a table of blueprints in the back of the room. Roehre believed that the man Sorenson saw was likely Lucius Blake, the driving force and primary founder of the Blake Opera House project. The medium also saw other spirits as they made their way through the low ceilings of the cellar, including a maid, perhaps a former hotel employee, a woman in an elegant red dress and a dandy gentleman who Sorenson believed may have died or been buried nearby after a robbery gone wrong. He reassured Roehre that the spirits that seemed to reside in the Old Stone Building were all amicable and none seemed malevolent in any way. Roehre was happy to hear her theory confirmed by Sorenson.

Despite all the strange occurrences in her business, Roehre still loves and feels a connection to the Old Stone Building. She prides herself on her knowledge of the building's historical past and the wonderful business she has created within it. Roehre doesn't mind sharing her space with a few stray spirits and wouldn't have it any other way.

CHAPTER 2

THE IVANHOE

Sitting at the southeast corner of Main and State Street is a unique and recognizable building that is known to locals as the Ivanhoe. From the outside, it evokes feelings of old-world European architecture. Its exterior is ornamented with solid white oak molding and large bay windows topped with pagoda-style roofs that lead up to spires. The sides of the building are adorned with large painted advertisements for Pabst beer. The overall aura of the building is unmistakably that of a pub, and so it has been since it was first erected.

A HISTORIC LOCATION

In 1890, in collaboration with the Pabst Brewing Company, Frank J. Mrkvicka (1843–1916) bought a small parcel of land for $2,500 and had his very own saloon built at 231 Main Street, designed and constructed by Milwaukeean Arnold Heiden (unknown). Mrkvicka was an upstanding Racinian and one of the charter members of the local Bohemian Society. He lived above the saloon with his wife, Anna (unknown), and his bright sixteen-year-old son, Ludwig (circa 1874–1892). A popular boy, Ludwig was well liked by his peers, instructors and his employer, Apnspitz and Koehn, a wholesale liquor company. Unfortunately, it was not long before tragedy struck. In early July 1892, Ludwig fell ill; he did not recover, and he succumbed to his illness in his bed at 3:00 a.m. on July 15, 1892. His funeral was held a few days later at their home and proved to be a large affair, with guests coming from all over the region, including Lieutenant Governor Charles Jonas, who led the service. After Ludwig's death, the Mrkvickas continued to move forward, operating their saloon until 1899, when another saloon owner, Charles Kannenberg (1865–1923), bought the property.

Under Kannenberg's ownership, the business operated as both a saloon and boardinghouse, attracting many interesting characters, including Thomas Dunham (unknown), who was suspected of having set fire to some Milwaukee properties owned by his employer, the J.I. Case Company, which had been owned by former Racine mayor Jerome Increase Case (1819 1891). In 1901, the establishment was taken over by Jens Norgaard (1872–1942), who renamed it as the Gem Hotel. Seven years later, he sold the business to James P. Jensen (unknown), who successfully managed it until passage of the Volstead Act in 1919. Better known as the Eighteenth Amendment, the act put a stop to the sale of alcoholic beverages. Jensen tried to continue on as a soft drinks parlor, but the business was unable to thrive and was eventually sold to Barney Richter (1890–1965) in 1921.

A former welterweight boxing champion and the owner of several popular Racine lunch carts, Richter created the Badger Hotel, later known as Richter's Hotel and Restaurant, which was known for its excellent German cuisine. Richter's occupied the building for nearly thirty-five years until the Theos family purchased it in the late 1950s. Under their ownership, the building was home to a variety of different restaurants, including the Ivanhoe (Greek restaurant), Zorba's, El Zarape and the Sanctuary, before again taking the name Ivanhoe. With the closing of the second Ivanhoe in 1986/87, the restaurant space remained vacant for sixteen years, while Theos owned the building and apartment space above.

In 2002, Doug Nicholson, an entrepreneur with a vision, set out to restore the restaurant space and create the newest incarnation Ivanhoe—the Ivanhoe Pub and Eatery. Filled with charming decor from eras past, its design is evocative of the building's storied past. Several of the light fixtures in the dining area were from when Richter's restaurant still resided there, including a pair of lamps from a horse-drawn hearse that were given to Richter as a gift for the grand opening of his restaurant. Also from Richter's restaurant is another lantern that hangs above the back of the restaurant—a recovered relic from a steamer known as the *Peck*, which exploded in Racine's harbor in 1913. Nicholson also collects his own unique decor to adorn the walls of his business, most of which are vintage memorabilia and advertisements designed to transport diners into a cozy and welcoming atmosphere.

Right: Richter's Restaurant, circa 1920s, exterior. *Property of Racine Heritage Museum, All Rights Reserved.*

Below: Richter's Restaurant, circa 1920s, interior. *Property of Racine Heritage Museum, All Rights Reserved.*

"Lady of the Saloon"

With his current success, however, it is one particular guest that Nicholson is quite familiar with, as he is sure that his business is haunted. Nicholson said that he isn't the only one who thinks so either and that many individuals—from patrons to his own employees—have had strange experiences of their own. Rumors say that a young woman—the "Lady of the Saloon"—allegedly haunts the halls of the historic building. Rumored to be the victim of a love triangle gone wrong, it is believed that she died in the building long ago, although no one knows when. She has appeared to employees on numerous occasions as a full-bodied apparition, and according to Nicholson, she might not be alone.

Most paranormal activity at the bar seems to take place after the bar has closed down for the night and in the morning before it has opened. According to an article by Michael Burke in the *Journal Times*, Leigh Ann Martinez, a former manager at the Ivanhoe, and former bartender Nic Savasta have both seen the ghostly silhouette of a young woman descending the staircase down to the first floor on separate occasions. Savasta said that after he saw the woman, he "didn't look that way for the rest of the night" and couldn't shake off the creepy feeling of being watched. Martinez has also seen the same woman pass through the kitchen doors in the back of the restaurant and has been around when smaller strange things have happened, like objects falling for no reason even when they aren't near anything that could knock them over.

One night, Martinez and Savasta were closing up the pub together when they both experienced something strange. After turning out the lights, Savasta came back up from the basement, but when the two went to check the security cameras to make sure everything was in order, they both were surprised to see a remaining light on in the basement. Savasta knew he had just turned that light out but marched back to the basement door with Martinez to check. When he reached out to open it, the door was locked. The door was never locked—in fact, the key to the basement door had been lost several years earlier. Martinez and Savasta both failed to get the door open and left Ivanhoe unable to turn off that last basement light. When the employees returned the next morning, however, they were surprised to find the very same door wide open. To this day, Martinez and Savasta cannot explain the incident.

According to the *Journal Times*, another bartender, Heather Coe, also encountered something strange in the basement. While she was alone in the cellar, she heard the sound of whistling. Coe froze, as she was certain that she was the only one down there. The whistling grew louder and louder, as if its source was advancing toward the frightened Coe, but when she turned to see who was whistling, there was no one there and the whistling inexplicably stopped.

These spirits don't confine themselves to only spooking Ivanhoe's employees at night, either. Nicholson arrived at his business early one morning to start preparing for the day when he spotted one of his employees out of the corner of his eye. He muttered a tired greeting to her, surprised she'd managed to make it to work before him, and after she responded, he moved on to continue with his work. A short while later, when Nicholson returned to the room, however, he ran into the same employee he had greeted moments earlier—who was just coming in for the morning. A surprised Nicholson asked her if she had gotten in earlier, but the employee admitted she was only just arriving now.

Another employee, Jeremie McDowell, has been bartending at Ivanhoe for the past eighteen years, and during his time in the building, he has had several strange experiences. The most frequent occurrence happens every so often when McDowell is locking up for the night. Right before he leaves, he said he sometimes hears a knocking—the same three knocks every time—in the corner above the stage. He also has seen doors open and close and been a witness to many unexplainable electronic malfunctions in the restaurant. As a longtime employee of the business, however, McDowell has had several more "memorable" experiences that he recounted in an interview.

Around fifteen years ago, Nicholson and McDowell were alone in the building one night after bar close when something bizarre happened. McDowell and Nicholson had just finished up work in the kitchen when they sat down to enjoy a beer in one of the restaurant's many booths. From the booth, the stained-glass window that looks out to the front door was visible. In the middle of their conversation, the two heard the door begin to open and turned to watch it opening. Moments later, the door slammed shut, a loud bang reverberating through the dining room. They got up from the booth to inspect the front door but found it tightly locked.

In a similar experience to Nicholson, about a decade ago, McDowell arrived to work early in the morning and was the first person there. He walked into the kitchen, past the walk-in cooler and was about to round the corner when he heard the voice of one of his female coworkers, clear as day, say, "Good morning," to him. When he came around the corner by the kitchen office, no one was there. McDowell was stumped. The spirits at Ivanhoe seemed to enjoy impersonating employees.

Another time, about six years earlier, McDowell grabbed McDonald's breakfast and headed down to Ivanhoe to watch a soccer game on a channel he didn't have at home. It was around 6:30 a.m. when he arrived and sat down at the left end of the bar in front of one of the TVs. He turned the TV on and the volume for it and began to munch and watch the game. Suddenly, the jukebox turned on and the speaker directly behind McDowell began to blast Billy Idol's "Eyes without a Face." McDowell leapt up from his seat, knocking the barstool to the ground in the process. Ten seconds of music played and then abruptly stopped. McDowell said the experience was by far the most memorable he has had at the bar. Later, he said, he and Nicholson reviewed the security footage and had a good laugh.

Though most of those who have experienced the presence of the spirits in Ivanhoe feel unthreatened, the spirits' origins are rumored to be somewhat dark in nature. Local medium Billy Givens of Spiritually Charmed believes that the spirits at the Ivanhoe are those of several prostitutes who were murdered by a client of theirs back in the building's days as a hotel and boardinghouse. The killer was allegedly known as "the Slasher." Givens suggested that the prostitutes who remained avenged their fallen sisters by murdering the killer and that pieces of his remains were found along Lake Michigan circa 1912. According to a *Racine Journal* article published in May 1912, the mutilated body of a man was found severed in half and missing his right leg above the knee. It was speculated that the unidentified man may have been cut in half by the ice, but no follow-up on the incident was ever published.

Even though he was physically gone, the murderer's negative presence can still be felt around the restaurant, according to Givens. He said that the negative energy was so strong it may have seeped over the boundaries of Ivanhoe's property onto the site of the former De Pizza Chef restaurant and contributed to the somewhat unsavory side hustle that was discovered at the restaurant in 2017. The site has a noticeable history of tragic mishaps. A gentleman known as William Schafer, who had been staying at the Gem Hotel in 1908, wandered off the site and down State Street and tried unsuccessfully to take his own life with a revolver shot to the head. In 1911, an intoxicated patron of Jensen's saloon fainted and struck his head against a large scale, causing a near fatal injury.

Givens isn't the only Racinian to talk about the potential of the ghosts of Ivanhoe as sex workers. While researching the location, several residents said that they had heard that one of the spirits was that of a courtesan who was involved in an unfortunate love triangle, which ended in her murder. An

EVP (electronic voice phenomenon) recorded by the TriCounty Paranormal Group in 2011 lends some credence to the theory of one or more prostitutes haunting the location. During their recording session, they caught a man's voice saying, "Put ten dollars on the bar," followed by a woman's voice responding, "We don't know you. You're not worthy." Nicholson suggested this EVP may have captured an echo of the site's former business as a brothel.

Finding evidence of Racine's darker underbelly in the late 1800s is difficult, as many avoided the subject, especially in an area where moral reform was a growing movement at the time. However, there is record of a young woman found wandering near the State Street bridge after having escaped being lured into brothel work, according to a *Journal Times* article from 1891. She was enticed by a help wanted ad in the newspaper that offered good and reputable work. When she discovered the true nature of the job, she fled. Again, State Street is mentioned in a 1907 *Racine Journal* article. A well-known businessman by the name of Edward Schowalter (1866–1940) was accused of keeping a brothel at his building on the east corner of State and Main Streets. This article also remarks that the buildings on the northwest corner of the same streets are "occupied by questionable resorts." Though the warrant was withdrawn after it was discovered that Schowalter was renting the building to someone else, this still suggests that the corner of State and Main Streets was a hotbed of scandalous activity at the time. Also, in 1912, James Jensen, the then-owner of the Gem Hotel, was ordered to pay a fine of ten dollars for being found at a "resort" that allegedly participated in human trafficking.

Though the ghosts at the Ivanhoe, whoever they may be, have a habit of spooking employees and causing trouble, Nicholson doesn't mind sharing his restaurant with them. It's just another part of Ivanhoe Pub & Eatery's unique atmosphere and allure.

CHAPTER 3

D.P. WIGLEY

S tanding at the intersection of Third Street and Wisconsin Avenue is a building seeping with age and history. From Wisconsin Avenue, three stories of the old Cream City brick building are visible, worn down and emblazoned with faded painted text across the bricks near the top of the building: "The D.P. Wigley Co." To the outside observer, it may look like the name of a business from a bygone era, but in fact, the business still houses D.P. Wigley. The building sports a peaked roof with a flat roofed addition and a wooden stoop that runs along the entire length of the business. The opposite side of the property faces the Root River, and from that side, the building looks quite different. According to the summer 2001 issue of the *Preservation Racine* newsletter, "the building rises up from a stone foundation along the banks of the Root River and climbs up the bluff up to the street," towering six stories above the water. The industrial building has always been a mill, and the grain chutes and old coal boiler within its walls speak to that history.

RACINE'S OLDEST MILL

Sometime between 1847 and 1849, the first city mill was built on the site where D.P. Wigley now stands. In 1872, it seems, the building was expanded or rebuilt to house the Emerson Company Linseed Oil Works, which was

Image showing the rear of D.P. Wigley and the Shoop Building from the Root River. *Property of Racine Heritage Museum, All Rights Reserved.*

D.P. Wigley, current day. *Author's collection.*

formed via a partnership between Thomas J. Emerson (1815–1909) and Henry S. Durand (1861–1929). It is said that the partnership didn't last long, however, as it was contentiously dissolved within a decade of its creation. After the end of his partnership with Durand, Emerson ran the company with his two sons, William (1851–1906) and Charles (1848–1897). Even in 1890, after they sold their business to the National Linseed Oil Company of Chicago, the family still stayed on in leadership. In 1899, it was again sold, this time to the National Linseed Oil Company of New Jersey. Linseed oil, which the company used the mill to produce, was one of the main ingredients used in paints prior to the popularization of latex and water-based paint. Unfortunately, growing flax was very taxing on soil, and as technology continued to advance, linseed oil was no longer as profitable of a product by the early 1900s.

In 1905, Welsh immigrant David Paynter Wigley (1856–1912) purchased the property and used the old mill to create the D.P. Wigley Company, which sold Ben Hur flour, seeds, twine, livestock feed and grain. After his death in 1912, his wife and widow, Jane Wigley (1861–1946), went on to continue managing the company. Current owners Mark and Christine Flynn purchased the property in 1998 and continued the mill's legacy, operating it as a small feed mill and selling birdseed, livestock feed, seeds, ready-mix concrete and other building materials. Now the building also houses Hop to It Brewing and Winemaking Supplies, a natural offshoot of its grain operations. To this day, it remains Racine's oldest continuously operating mill.

Singing Specters

Early one Sunday morning, Mark Flynn thought he heard a soft singing coming from beneath the docks outside his business. He went outside to locate the source of the strange singing, but finding himself unable to do so, he went back to work. After working for a short while, Flynn was aware of a soft singing once more. He listened closer this time, realizing he couldn't seem to understand any of the words, as if the song was being sung in a foreign language. Flynn had almost brushed off the experience until the following day, when a construction worker who was working on the nearby construction project at State Street and Wisconsin Avenue popped in. He asked Flynn if he'd heard the news—while they had been digging up the

Anne Stanford's tombstone, cemented into the wall of the Shoop Building, 1983. *Property of Racine Heritage Museum, All Rights Reserved.*

road, they had discovered the old gravestone of a Welsh woman buried beneath the street. The body of the woman was never found though.

According to further investigation into the site, no cemeteries—public or private—ever seem to have existed at the corners of Wisconsin and State. The headstone ended up belonging to Anne Stanford, wife of mariner Edward Stanford. Anne was a native of Wales. After looking through the city's censuses and finding no record of Anne or Edward, research librarian Virginia Hefferon said she believed it was likely that the couple had been transients, just passing through Racine at the time of Anne's death.

According to her headstone, she died on May 24, 1852, just four months from her thirty-first birthday.

Not wanting to disturb Anne's grave any more than they already had, it was decided to keep the tombstone close to where it was originally found. At first, workers placed the tombstone into the wall of a vault in the storm sewer beneath the road. The stone, around eighteen inches wide and four feet long, was cemented into the wall. It is accessible from the basement of the Shoop Building, which stands at the southeast corner of State Street and Wisconsin Avenue. To this day, in the alleyway behind the Shoop Building and near the loading docks at D.P. Wigley, some say they have heard a woman singing in an unfamiliar language. Most often, the voice can be heard around three o'clock in the morning, well after bar close in the area.

PART II

LEGENDS OF THE LAKEFRONT

The following locations are a part of the Live Towerview neighborhood of Racine. This neighborhood sits against Lake Michigan, just south of downtown Racine. It is home to many of Racine's most significant historic buildings and within its boundaries holds more history than most neighborhoods. Many noteworthy sites, including the former homes of many prominent Racine citizens, are located throughout Live Towerview. However, the neighborhood also has a rather strange past. Ron Helmick, the founder of Racine Paranormal Investigators, likened Lake Michigan to dousing rods—the water acts like a conduit for spiritual energy.

PIONEER CEMETERY

Located in the area surrounded by Thirteenth, Fourteenth, College and Villa Streets was Racine's first official cemetery, established in 1842. Created during the pioneer era of early Racine, the property became known as the "Old Cemetery." Telling of the time when it was established, the first man buried in the cemetery died of tuberculosis, a disease that commonly plagued the area. Little is known about the cemetery itself, but its eventual fate was well recorded.

Just ten short years later, it was decided that the cemetery had reached its capacity and that the site would be better suited for the future Third Ward School. By then, several hundred bodies had already been buried in the Old Cemetery, and they would have to be exhumed before construction could begin on the school. They would need to be moved to nearby Evergreen Cemetery or the newer Mound Cemetery in West Racine. In 1853, an announcement written by City Clerk J. Redburn (unknown) was printed in Racine's newspaper: "Notice is hereby given to all those having an interest, that in accordance with a resolution passed by the City Council of the City of Racine, November 7th, 1852, all the bodies buried in the Old Cemetery must be resolved by the 1st day of January 1854."

The Third Ward School was constructed due to overcrowding in Racine's original schools, along with two additional new schools, known as the Fourth and Fifth Ward Schools. The money was raised for their construction in 1855, and they were completed in 1856. By July 1900, the former Third, Fourth and Fifth Ward Schools would come to be known as Winslow, Janes and Garfield Elementary Schools, respectively. All three original buildings were designed by Lucas Bradley (1809–1899), who happened to be the brother-in-law of Horatio Gates Winslow (1820–1893), a popular superintendent of the ward schools and the Third Ward School's eventual namesake. The schools were constructed in the popular Italianate style and made from Cream City brick and limestone. Forty-three years later, at the turn of the century, James G. Chandler (1856–1924), a Racine architect also known for his work on the Shoop Building and former Racine YMCA in downtown Racine, made expansions to all three schools. Thus, very little of the schools' original exteriors remain. The new buildings had a castle-like appearance and were in use for over a century and a half, going through many more additions during their lifespan.

Unfortunately, during the construction of homes near the Third Ward—now Winslow—School, homeowners began to find bones on their properties. Some Racine residents who had loved ones buried in the Old Cemetery were unable to locate their relatives' remains in either of Racine's newer cemeteries. It appeared that during the exhumation of bodies in 1853, they may have missed a few. The number of bones found on and near the school's lot is unknown, but reportedly, two complete skeletons were found over the course of the Winslow School's history. Bones were occasionally found in the schoolyard by students, so much so that the children affectionately referred to the water of the old water pump on the lot as "skeleton juice."

Over the years of its operation, staff and students at the school have claimed to have witnessed several paranormal occurrences. Frequently, staff has said that they felt like they were being watched while completely alone in a classroom or that they passed through unusually cold spots while walking through the halls. Many orbs have also been spotted throughout the building. After receiving new computers in 2009, students were playing with the new webcam feature and taking pictures of themselves in the computer lab. However, after going through the photos, a teacher observed a young girl in the background of one of the pictures whom she did not recognize. The girl had long dark hair in two braids and looked as if she was wearing a dress made from animal hide. The teacher was about to send the photo to one of her colleagues

Winslow Elementary School, current day. *Author's collection.*

Rear view of the Ascension Wisconsin Avenue campus, showing some of the oldest parts of the building. *Author's collection.*

when the computer crashed and everything on it was lost. The school officially closed in 2005.

Now an empty building, the old Winslow School sits behind the oldest buildings of the Wisconsin Avenue campus of Ascension All Saints Hospital, located at 1320 Wisconsin Avenue. The paranormal occurrences that plagued Winslow School seem to have seeped over the boundaries of the lot, as many have also experienced strange happenings while on the hospital property. Staff have heard disembodied voices and seen ominous shadowy figures roaming the hall while alone. A third-shift employee was alone in the kitchen when suddenly and without explanation, all of the appliances began to go off and the room was filled with the sight of flashing lights and sound of many alarms ringing. Then, all the power went out. A different third-shift employee said that oftentimes on their deathbeds, patients would claim to see Jesus or other ethereal beings. When patients did pass, staff opened all the doors and windows in the room to make sure that no souls became trapped in the hospital. Nearly all of the employees who have reported strange happenings worked third shift and agreed that the hospital kitchen was a hotspot between 1:00 and 4:00

Front view of the Ascension Wisconsin Avenue campus. *Property of Racine Heritage Museum, All Rights Reserved.*

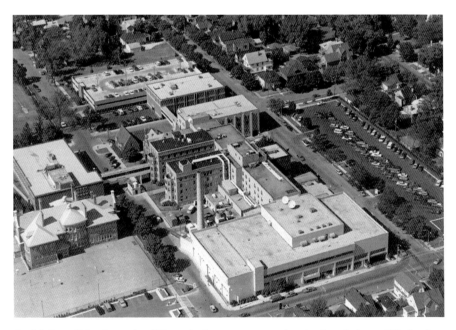

Aerial view of the Ascension Wisconsin Avenue campus, showing its relation to Winslow's campus. *Property of Racine Heritage Museum, All Rights Reserved.*

a.m. Patients, too, have reported bizarre experiences during their overnight stays, including hearing creepy sounds and disembodied voices and seeing handprints and writing appear on windows that had previously been clean. Patients also have had the showers and sinks in their private bathrooms turn on and off without explanation.

LAKESIDE BURIAL

The Old Cemetery is not Live Towerview's only former cemetery. Along the lakefront across from the current-day site of the DeKoven Center, located between DeKoven Avenue and Twenty-First Street, was the Evergreen Cemetery. Dedicated on June 12, 1851, the cemetery received its first burial in 1852. At the time, the DeKoven Center was an all-boys' school known as Racine College and would share a border with Evergreen Cemetery on the southeast corner of the lot. Evergreen itself butted up against the cliffside over Lake Michigan, where Roosevelt Park and the city's sewage plant exist today.

Evergreen Cemetery was not in use for long, and many of the records of burials there were destroyed in the infamous "Blaze of 1882." Mound Cemetery, which was established in West Racine in 1852, was reportedly the preferred burial ground of many Racine residents. Evergreen subsequently fell into disrepair and neglect, and the property was deemed a nuisance. In 1866, it was sold to Daniel Bull (1828–1899), who became responsible for exhuming and relocating all the bodies on the property. Unfortunately, out of the potential hundreds of bodies interred on the site, only seventy-six were recovered.

While in disrepair, the cemetery also became the victim of vandals and grave robbers. Vandals defaced the headstones that remained, and medical students from Milwaukee and Chicago used some of the remaining corpses for cadavers. Racine College students also explored the property, and on one harrowing occasion, a student was injured when part of

ORDER OF EXERCISES,

AT THE DEDICATION OF THE

EVERGREEN CEMETERY,

AT RACINE, WISCONSIN,

THURSDAY, JUNE 12th, 1851.

1937
1851
86

FIRST.—Remarks by one of the Committee.

SECOND.—Reading of the Scriptures, by REV. MR. McNEIL.

THIRD.—Opening Prayer, by REV. MR. HOPKINS.

FOURTH.—Singing ; Prepared for the occasion.

HYMN.

Holy Father! wilt thou hearken,
To the songs we now would raise—
Lowly, solemn would we have them,
Breathing words of sweetest praise;
Praise, that thou hast granted to us,
This fair spot wherein to lay
The loved forms of those whose spirits
From our earth have passed away.

Praise, that 'midst the leaves and blossoms,
They may take their dreamless sleep;
Praise, that we, sad, weary mourners,
Have a fitting place to weep;
Here our hands delight to train
Flowers that, though on graves they flourish,
Will not bloom, nor fade in vain.

For a floweret's faintest whisper,
Of a better land doth speak—
Of a land where sorrow comes not,
Where no tears course down the cheek;
And its dying accents murmur,
Pine not, though fond ties are riven —
For each flower on earth that fadeth,
Fairer, brighter blooms in heav'n.

Holy Father! wilt thou hearken,
To the prayer we now would raise!
Grant that when our days are numbered,
We may join the songs of praise,
Round thine everlasting throne—
Grant that in those blissful mansions,
We may meet all—ALL OUR OWN.

FIFTH.—Address by REV. MR. ROLLINSON.

SIXTH.—Singing of the following

ODE.

This holy ground beneath our feet,
Near where the Lake's blue waters move,
Where Nature's quiet beauties meet,
Shall be the home of those we love.

Above their couch shall flow'rets bloom—
Dear, precious flowers, that droop and die,
'Tis fit that ye should wreathe the tomb,
Where those we best have loved, shall lie.

But they shall wake when o'er the earth
Time's last receding wave shall roll;

Shall share in an immortal birth,
The changeless spring-time of the soul.

Then let us learn to bear aright
Life's weary weight of pain and care,
Till, with our heavenly home in sight,
This last and dreamless couch we share.

Oh! let us see thy glory here,
Our Father! and we'll kiss the rod;
We leave ourselves, and all most dear,
With Thee, our Savior and our God!

SEVENTH.—Dedicatory Prayer, by REV. MR. HUMPHREY.

EIGHTH.—Singing, "The Orphan's Prayer."

HYMN.

I love to stay where my mother sleeps,
And gaze on each star as it twinkling peeps,
Through that bending willow which lonely weeps,
O'er my mother's grave, o'er my mother's grave.

I love to kneel on the green turf there,
Afar from the scene of my daily care,
And breathe to my Savior my evening prayer,
O'er my mother's grave, o'er my mother's grave.

I still remember how oft she led,
And knelt me by her, as with God she plead,
That I might be His, when the clod spread
O'er my mother's grave, o'er my mother's grave.

I love to think how 'neath the ground,
She slumbers in death as a captive bound,
She'll slumber no more when the trump shall sound,
O'er my mother's grave, o'er my mother's grave.

NINTH.—Benediction, by REV. MR. McNEIL.

W. R. Perry, Fancy Job Printer, Commercial Advertiser Office, Racine.

The 1851 "Order of Exercises" at the Dedication of Evergreen Cemetery.
Property of Racine Heritage Museum, All Rights Reserved.

the lakeside embankment fell out from beneath him. After his rescue, his peers discovered a coffin jutting out of the side of the land and pried the bottom of it open. A complete skeleton was discovered inside, and the school took possession of the remains and burned them. Coffins protruding from the cliffside and bodies falling into the lake were both reportedly commonplace, according to an article in the *Racine Review* published in June 1928.

The fate of the abandoned Evergreen Cemetery lot was brought up again in the late 1920s, when a battle over ownership began. Both Racine College and the Town of Mount Pleasant had different ideas for how to take care of the ill-kept site. The college wanted to clean up the property and leave it be, since it shared a border with the school and there had been little supervision of the site. Mount Pleasant wished to take ownership of the land and turn it into a public park that would add beauty to the landscape, as a sewage plant was soon to be built nearby. Although the legal battle would not be completely resolved, a large portion of the site, ravaged by erosion and the lack of maintenance, eventually collapsed into Lake Michigan, leaving little behind.

Sand from the nearby sewage plant was often used for construction, and in 1984, some was hauled to a lot on the 5300 block of Wind Point Road for the construction of a new home. The construction crew, however, found a human skull, pelvis and other human bones in the pile of sand. The bones proved to be over one hundred years old, and it was speculated that they were remnants from the Evergreen Cemetery. The shocked homeowners likely thought that would be their last encounter with century-old human remains, but thirty-three years later, they discovered that was not the case. In late November 2017, the owners began a project to widen their driveway. While they were digging, a human jawbone with several teeth still attached, several ribs, an arm bone and additional bone fragments were found. The Racine County sheriff's office was contacted to determine if these bones were also from Evergreen. It was found that they likely had been from the same sand deposit that had been used on the lot some three decades earlier.

DeKoven Center, current day. *Author's collection.*

Apparitions—like a woman wearing a wedding dress wandering the woods and a couple dancing in the gymnasium of the DeKoven Center—have been reported. Visitors have also reported strange cold spots and apparitions in the garden and surrounding grounds. A former resident of the DeKoven Center gatehouse often heard footsteps running up and down the stairs to her apartment, the unexplained music of a flute and the sound of doors being slammed shut. Also, near the gymnasium, she recorded hearing the sounds of gym shoes squeaking and basketballs being bounced on the wooden floors while she walked her dog around the empty property at night. She even claimed that the presence at the DeKoven Center tied both her shoelaces and vacuum cord in knots once.

The resident of a nearby home, only two blocks away from the property, also reported hearing footsteps and doors opening and closing after she and her family had already gone to bed for the night. She and her husband also saw the apparition of an old woman standing in their bedroom doorway and saw what they believed to be a Union soldier in their basement.

Her son and other homeowners in the neighborhood have also apparently seen the soldier's apparition around the area. Similarly, neighbors have also experienced phenomena, such as electrical appliance malfunctions, doors opening and closing without explanation and the unnerving feeling of being watched while alone at night. The history of this neighborhood may contribute to the paranormal experiences of the residents of other nearby homes.

CHAPTER 4
THE DURAND MANSION AND MASONIC TEMPLE

Standing tall on the corner of Main and Tenth Streets is a three-story Italianate mansion whose very presence commands respect. Italianate design was most popular in the mid- to late nineteenth century. This home, known as the Durand Mansion, was deemed "Racine's most important Italianate mansion" by architectural historian H. Russell Zimmerman. The front entrance features two gorgeous bronze doors, each weighing about one ton. All around the house are many tall windows, bay windows, porches and a porte-cochère—a term used to describe a porch roof that projects over a driveway. The gently sloping, low pitched roofs atop the home feature wide overhanging eaves with decorative brackets and a gorgeous cupola at the top. Within the home there are eleven fireplaces, each of which is completely unique and made from various mediums, including wrought iron, wood, tile and even Carrara marble.

The wood paneling inside the home is made from Philippine mahogany. Experts say each panel matches so well that it must have all come from the same tree. Not all of the woodwork in the home is Philippine mahogany; some other woods used in the construction include vermillion walnut, oak and French white ivory. Behind the mansion is the equally wondrous Masonic Temple, constructed in a style reminiscent of ancient Egyptian architecture. The Cream City brick from the mansion blends almost seamlessly into the custom-made yellow brick of the temple. Together, the two buildings create the Masonic Center. Although the Masonic Center is not yet in the National Register of Historic Places, it is considered a key property in Racine's Southside Historic District.

The Masonic Center, current day. *Author's collection.*

FROM THE DURAND MANSION TO THE MASONIC CENTER

The Durand Mansion was built in 1855–56 for Henry Durand (1817–1899), a wealthy local businessman. The architect, who is believed to be Lucas Bradley, is also responsible for many other prominent nineteenth-century Racine buildings, including the Blake Opera House. Henry Durand first came to Racine from Hartford, Connecticut, in 1843. Durand lived in the home with his wife, Caroline (1817–1870); their four daughters, Frances (1850–1936), Caroline (1846–unknown), Alida (1856–1943) and Helen (1858–1902); and three servants, Edward Hammond (unknown), Mary Williams (1823–1882) and Mary Griffin (unknown). Williams is buried with the Durands at Mound Cemetery, having worked for them almost her entire life.

Durand, a jack-of-all-trades, was known for being an insurance agent for Etna Insurance; one of the main investors and first president of the Racine, Janesville and Mississippi Railroad; a city planner for LaCrosse, Wisconsin; and the vice president of the Racine Commercial Bank and the Racine

County Bank, as well as owning five "first-class vessels" on Lake Michigan for his shipping and trading business. While he was an insurance agent, Durand was responsible for writing one of the first insurance policies in Racine and did claims adjusting for one of Milwaukee's largest fires.

Wendy Spencer, the event coordinator of the Masonic Center and keeper of the home's history, believes the home may have even been used as a hiding spot during the Underground Railroad era. Durand, a notable abolitionist and member of an abolitionist church—the First Presbyterian Church, a nearby and confirmed Underground Railroad station—had several vessels on Lake Michigan, one of which went exclusively between Racine and Canada, the final destination of many of the former enslaved peoples escaping to freedom. Spencer said that she would like to locate the records that show how many individuals boarded in Racine versus how many got off in Canada, suspecting the two numbers likely wouldn't match. A strange and hidden crawlspace in the home's basement also seems to suggest that Spencer's theory is correct.

The home is no stranger to death, as Mary Williams, the head housekeeper for the Durands, passed away in the house. Durand's young daughter Caroline also passed away in the house, and Durand's wife died in the home after a long, mysterious illness that is now believed to have been cancer. After Mrs. Caroline Durand's death in 1870, Durand married Gertrude Whipple (1847–1874) in 1873, and he and his new wife had a child together about one year after they were married. Sadly, their baby passed away shortly after childbirth, and Durand's new wife died one week later due to complications from the birth. In 1891, Durand sold his home and moved to Chicago and passed away on March 14, 1899.

Otis W. Johnson (1855–1926) became the new owner of the property and also founded the Racine-based Fish Brother Wagon Company. Additionally, he went on to become the vice president of the Racine Tool and Machine Company, and in 1902, he was elected to the Wisconsin State Senate and chose to move to the capital with his wife and four daughters, leaving behind his home.

The next owner was Frederick Robinson (1863–1919), who purchased the home in 1903 and moved in with his wife, Lillian Bull Robinson (1861–1937), and their two children, Bessie (1891–1977) and Stephen (1889–1941). At the time, Robinson was the vice president of the J.I. Case Company, and his wife's father, Stephen Bull (1822–1913), was one of the four original founders. Ultimately, Robinson made many of the interior changes to the historic home that remain visible to this day. Robinson had plumbing, new

The Durand family portraits on the fireplace mantel. *Author's collection.*

heating and electricity added into the home. When replacing the flooring on the first floor, he hired the Johnson brothers to put in the beautiful new herringbone floor. Later, the Johnson brothers would go into the business of floorcare products, becoming the internationally known Johnson's Wax Company. It is estimated that while Robinson lived in the home, at least $100,000 was spent on decorations and renovations, many of which were in the popular art nouveau style.

When he died in 1919, Robinson made a provision in his will that stated that the property should be sold for $60,000, but if the Masons were interested in buying the home for "temple purposes" and would still preserve the integrity of the property, they could purchase the mansion for half that amount. Robinson himself was a part of the local Masonic lodge.

On May 29, 1920, the Masons received the deed to the Robinson family home. In 1922, the Masons began construction on the back addition to the home, which would serve as the new Masonic Temple. They commissioned Chicago architect Edmund B. Funston (1868–1933), also a member of the Masonic lodge, to design it in an Egyptian style, a popular design trend at the time due to the recent discovery of King Tutankhamun's tomb and

The Masonic Center parlor, current day. *Author's collection.*

the Egypt-mania phenomenon that followed. The cornerstone to the new addition was laid on May 27, 1922, and the Masons had a celebratory parade from their old temple to their new home. The parade was even recorded to be shown at a local theater later on. The building's formal dedication took place on June 30, 1923.

Two beautiful theater-style lodge rooms, a grand ballroom, a dining hall and a kitchen make up a majority of the addition. Within the halls, relics are featured in display cases, like former Mason William Horlick Jr.'s (1875– 1940) souvenirs from his trip to Egypt in 1902. Also on display in one of the upper rooms is a statue of a life-sized white horse and knight, bearing the Christian flag, meant to represent Jacques DeMolay (1243–1314), the last grandmaster of the Knights Templar.

In 1943, the Masons also bought the mansion next door to the Durand Mansion, which was built by William T. Lewis (1840–1915) of the Mitchell and Lewis Wagon Company. In 1967, the Masons had the old home demolished to make way for the parking lot that now stands to the right of the Durand Mansion. The Masons have also done some renovation to the home over the years, lightening the woodwork, refurnishing and redecorating certain areas. They hosted an open house on March 27, 1960, to showcase their new changes. The open house marked the end of three years of work on the building. In 1998, for the Masons' 150th anniversary, the 1922 cornerstone on the addition was opened and new artifacts were placed inside.

Currently, the Masonic Center operates as Belle City Lodge #92. Wendy Spencer, a lifelong member of the organization, takes responsibility for much of the care of the building as a historic site. The labyrinth of rooms that make up the mansion and adjoining temple are decorated with an array of vintage and antique items, many of which were acquired by Spencer herself through thrifting, antiquing and donation.

GHOSTS OF THE PAST

The Durand Mansion is said to be haunted by many ghosts, but Spencer isn't disturbed by their presence and has said that the "house gives me a great deal of peace." Many mediums have visited the Masonic Center, and with each new visit, Spencer says that she has learned more about the spirits she and the Masons share their building with.

Upon a walkthrough with one of the mediums, Spencer was told that while she was walking through the main house, she was followed by the entity of a gentleman who seemed to be upset. The medium told Spencer that he wanted them to go into "his" building. At first, Spencer was puzzled, until the medium revealed his name started with the letters "FUN." Spencer quickly realized she must have been referring to Funston, the architect of the addition. They moved on to do a walkthrough of the temple, and the spirit seemed to calm down until they entered one of the theater-style meeting rooms. The medium turned to Spencer and told her that Funston was again upset and demanded to know why they had covered "his door." Spencer couldn't think of any doors in the room that had ever been covered until the medium pointed to the stage. "He's pointing to the stage floor." Spencer then remembered that there had once been a trapdoor leading to storage space beneath the stage. After the stage had been recarpeted, the builders decided to just leave the door covered, as it was no longer being used.

As their tour came to an end, Spencer and the medium retired to the front parlor to talk. While chatting, the medium looked behind Spencer and informed her that another presence had entered the room. She described the appearance of the new man as well as his protective feelings toward Spencer. She immediately felt that it must have been Mr. Durand, who was always known to be protective of his wife and daughters. Durand's presence seemed to ward off Funston's and replace his more negative energy with a calmer and warmer feeling.

During an event hosted in the mansion, Spencer met a new friend and yet another medium. She was walking through the upstairs, which was currently off-limits to guests, when she came across two women in one of the bedrooms. Upon trying to kindly tell them that the area they were in was not currently open to the public, Spencer found a hand in her face and was shushed. The other woman in the room sheepishly explained that her friend who had shushed Spencer, Caroline Clapper, was a medium and was communicating with someone in the room. Interested, Spencer sat down and waited until Clapper was finished. After a moment, the medium turned to Spencer and pointed to her own chest: "I have a little girl in here with me, and she hurts right here and she says her chest is real tight. It hurts." Spencer stared in disbelief, knowing that Caroline—the Durands' daughter—likely passed after a bout of pneumonia. The medium wasn't finished, however.

"She wants to know where her like-sister is." Clapper said, "Her like-sister just turned fourteen." Spencer wasn't sure what Clapper meant until she added, "Her like-sister wears a blue dress and white apron." Spencer's own granddaughter used to portray Caroline, wearing a blue dress and white apron, during tours of the home. When her granddaughter used to visit, she was much younger. Spencer said she used to love running around, playing with someone no one else could see. She would even sit on the floor and play with some of the old toys, talking with her unseen playmate. Occasionally, she'd tell her grandmother that there was a lady who was cleaning the home or to be quiet as the man in the library was trying to read. At the time that Spencer encountered Clapper, her granddaughter had indeed celebrated her fourteenth birthday one week prior. Perhaps her granddaughter had seen Williams, the former housekeeper, or Mr. Robinson or even his son, who was also said to be seen sitting in the armchair in the library, reading.

In 2014, before founding the Racine Paranormal Investigators, Ron Helmick was DJing a wedding that was being hosted at the Masonic Center. As he was finishing up for the night, he packed up his equipment and started up his old van. He went to back out of his spot but quickly slammed on his brakes when he spotted a man in his passenger mirror walking behind the car. The man was tall, shadowy and appeared to be in a trench coat and fedora. He passed out of the view of one mirror and into the next. Helmick quickly got out of his car to apologize for almost hitting the man, but by the time he got out and looked around, the gentleman was nowhere to be seen. The parking lot was empty. Afterward, while talking with Spencer about his experience, she suggested it might have been the spirit of Mr. Robinson.

CHAPTER 5

THE HUGHES HOUSE

Sitting on the corner of the street across from Lake Michigan is the large and spacious beautiful Queen Anne home known as the Hughes House. The house is painted a pale blue, and the lawn and adjoining yard on its left are well manicured. The house looks old, very old, but well cared for and inviting. The porch looks cozy, and the windows all around the property look like they would let in plenty of sunlight, bathing the house in a warm glow every afternoon. This home has passed through the hands of some of Racine's greatest men, been an apartment building to many and was even a bed-and-breakfast. Nowadays, it sits quietly, once again a single-family home, as it was originally built.

HISTORY OF THE HOME

In 1899, William A. Hughes (1857–1911) had the Hughes House built for him and his wife, Esther Hughes (1859–1925). Hughes was a Racine native and had started his career as a humble telegraph operator at the Racine Junction of the St. Paul Railroad. Through hard work and dedication, he managed to advance through various positions until he became a general agent of the Rock Island and Pacific Railroad Company, basing his office out of Milwaukee, while continuing to live in Racine. Notably, Hughes also played for the city of Racine's first professional baseball team and was said to have been one of their best catchers.

In 1902, Hughes decided to sell his newly built home and ended up passing on the property to William Mitchell Lewis (1869–1927) and his wife, Edith Lewis (1869–1955). Lewis was well known in the city, as he was one of the founders of the local company the Mitchell Motor Car Company, formerly the Mitchell Wagon Company. Lewis stayed in the home longer than Hughes, eventually selling it in 1921 to yet another prominent Racinian—Louis Vance (1872–1952) and his wife, Lillie Vance (1873–1947). At the time, Vance was the vice president of the Racine Rubber Company, later to be known as the Ajax Rubber Company. Vance was also considered one of Racine's pioneer industrialists and served as the director of the Racine County Relief Department, director of the First National Bank and Trust Company and member of the Masons and a charter member of the Racine Rotary Club.

In 1927, the home was sold to local couple, Thomas (1888–1959) and Helen Kearney (1888–1945). Thomas was a practicing lawyer, but not much else is known about their time in the home. However, on August 2, 1945, tragedy struck and a fire broke out in the home. Unfortunately, Helen was trapped in the master bedroom of the home and suffered serious burns,

The Hughes House, current day. *Author's collection.*

despite having been rescued from the blaze. The following day, August 3, 1945, she died of her wounds at St. Mary's Hospital.

In 1947, the home was converted from a single-family home and divided into apartments for rent, and from this point on information on the home and its tenants seems to fade into obscurity. Later, in 1992, the home reappeared when local couple Russel and Sandra Larson purchased the house and began work on restoring it back to its former glory. At first, they continued to rent to tenants but eventually worked on converting the first two floors back into a single-family home. Sadly, Russel Larson passed away in the master bedroom of his home on July 30, 2002, after having battled a long illness.

In 2003, Sandra Larson sold the home to Dan Dashner and Mike Reynolds, who had plans to open the home as a bed-and-breakfast and did so in 2006. The two were impressed by the gorgeous and well-cared-for interior, and Dashner said of it, "They did a fantastic job restoring it." Still, the two men had more work to do before opening the home as a tourist destination. While they owned the property, Dashner and Reynolds did their best to restore the exterior of the home, which had been heavily altered throughout the years, to its earliest known appearance. However, due to the recession and other financial difficulties, by 2015 the bed-and-breakfast was closed and the property was once again on the market. In August 2016, the home was sold to its new current owners.

What Goes Bump in the Night

Former owners Dashner and Reynolds have both claimed to witness multiple occurrences that lend credence to the theory that the Hughes House is, in fact, haunted. Dashner's first experience occurred over three nights. Each night, he would place his glass on his bedside table before settling in to sleep, yet each night at 3:15 a.m., he was awakened by the sound of his glass falling off the table and smashing on the ground. The third night, he was careful to set the glass far from the edge of the table and his own reach, yet at 3:15 a.m., he was awake again. This time, he had been startled into consciousness by the glass shattering on the floor, shards ending up as far as twelve feet away.

Early one morning, Dashner was loading the dishwasher when he saw what he described as a misty white and formless shape float past him and toward the bathroom. Reynolds, who was in the bathroom at the time, described what he saw differently—to him, what floated toward him looked like an actual man. Then the man disappeared into thin air. Both men have also heard what they described as "definite and deliberate" footsteps in the west wing of the home. While work was being done on the home in 2004, Rob Tomes, a carpenter Dashner and Reynolds had hired, had a frightening experience. He became spooked when he saw someone move down the hallway into one of the small rear bedrooms while he was alone, working on the second-floor landing. He thought someone had broken in, but no one was there.

Joyce Wilde, a previous renter of the home before it was opened as a bed-and-breakfast, said she had seen what she believed to be Russel Larson's ghost in the kitchen of the home on multiple occasions. She said, "It looked like him and had the outline of his head and face and was the same height." According to Wilde, whenever changes were being made to the property, she would see an increase in paranormal activity, as if the spirits were curious about what was going on. After hearing about others' experiences on the property, Dashner decided to keep a journal of any occurrences that guests staying at the bed-and-breakfast reported to him. The whereabouts of said journal, however, are unknown.

Other claims that the Hughes House is haunted can be found as far back as a 1998 news article in the *Journal Times*. In the article, Russel Larson was interviewed on the history of his home and said that although he didn't believe in ghosts, his daughter and tenant Jessica Larson did. She said she felt a presence in the upstairs apartments and had heard strange disembodied voices while alone in her own apartment. Charity Ramirez, an earlier tenant, echoed Jessica's beliefs. Unfortunately, Ramirez's experiences were more negative. Ramirez had two different cats vanish while living there, and two more met tragic and bizarre fates—one was killed when a heavy chair fell over on it when no one was home, and the other died after an open window suddenly fell down onto it. Ramirez also said she felt someone sit down next to her on her waterbed in the middle of the night, able to feel the dent in the mattress created by the entity's weight beside her.

In later years, Jessica discussed some of her other experiences while living in her apartment within the Hughes House. Although she was aware of the tragic death of Helen Kearney and the home's history, she wasn't afraid of any ghosts that may reside there, as she thought of them more as imprints of energy that was leftover from past people and events, not as sentient consciousnesses. Jessica said she would occasionally see things out of the corner of her eye but had just dismissed the experiences until the day she saw a shadow walking past the window on the northeast wall of her room. She was shocked, as the shadow was so definite, and the silhouette appeared to be that of a woman wearing a long gown. It was the middle of the day, and the room was bright and sunny.

While living there, Jessica ended up getting a roommate who, after experiences of her own, hung crosses on each wall, only to find them on the ground later. After witnessing one of the crosses fall off the wall in front of her, Jessica's roommate would no longer spend the night in the apartment if she knew she would be alone. Instead, she opted to sleep over at her parents' house. Her roommate even suggested getting the apartment exorcised, although they never did. During her time at the apartment, Jessica also got a kitten, which she named Storm. Storm made a habit of following her and her roommate around the house whenever they were there and did the same to visitors. On many occasions, Jessica said Storm would walk around the apartment, staring up into the air as if she was following someone. Sometimes, she would suddenly stop and hiss at the unseen presence, puffing up and running away to hide behind the bathroom toilet or under one of their beds. She thought there might have been two energies in the home— one that Storm seemed to be fond of and another that she feared.

One March, Jessica and her roommate decided to go down to New Orleans for Mardi Gras and asked friends Matt Scheck and Mike Schubring to watch over the apartment and cat-sit for them. While there, the two men had experiences of their own. Both Scheck and Schubring consider themselves to be skeptical when it comes to the supernatural, but after just one week in the apartment, both men felt forced to admit that their experiences went beyond the explainable.

While Scheck was alone in the apartment, his first experiences were easy to brush off. While in the kitchen and living room, he heard what he thought was someone whispering his name in his ear. At first, he thought perhaps it could have been him overhearing someone from one of the other apartments on the floor below, but it kept happening. Each time, it seemed too clear and distinct. Any time he came near the living room fireplace, he felt a chill but chalked it up to the flue being open and causing a draft—until he heard his name again. But this time it wasn't just a whisper in his ear—it was as if someone said his name right in front of him. After a while, he started to feel like he was being watched. Unbeknownst to Scheck at the time, Schubring was having similar experiences while alone in the apartment. While petting Storm on the floor in Jessica's room, Schubring was sure he heard someone whisper his name. He thought it could have been Mr. and Mrs. Larson talking about him housesitting from below, but the more he thought about it, the more unlikely it seemed. They were two floors below him, and the only word he had heard at all was his name.

Scheck recalled noticing Storm's odd behavior around the apartment, saying while they were staying there, she would occasionally take off after something and follow it through the home when nothing was there. One night, Scheck lay on his stomach on the couch, drifting off to sleep, when he felt Storm jump up onto him, walk up his legs and settle on his back. Scheck didn't care and let her stay on top of him until it started to feel as if she was getting heavier and heavier, pressing down into his back. He couldn't shake the feline and found it incredibly hard to move. As Scheck shouted for her to get off of him and craned his neck to see, he was shocked to see Storm not on top of him but in the corner of the room. She was staring directly at him and then arched her back and hissed in his direction, running out of the living room. Scheck leaped off the couch, feeling the weight lift off him, and found himself shaken. He decided to cool off with a smoke break outside by the lakefront. After he returned from the outdoors, he decided he'd try sleeping in one of the bedrooms but described being too tense to sleep and hearing tapping on the windows— as if someone was out there, watching him.

One of the times Schubring stayed overnight, he decided to use Jessica's bed, which at the time was just a mattress and box spring pushed up against the wall. While he lay in bed trying to fall asleep, Schubring said he felt Storm jump up on the bed and walk between his body and the wall. He rolled over to pet her, only to find nothing there. He knew he would have felt her jump off the bed or heard her land on the floor if she left, especially since he'd felt her get on the bed in the first place. He described the incident as puzzling at the time.

After so many strange happenings, Scheck and Schubring both ended up staying the night in the apartment. Nothing unusual seemed to happen the whole night, but the relief didn't last long. Upon waking up, Schubring asked Scheck what he'd been up to the night before—he'd woken up in the middle of the night to hear Scheck walking up and down the hallway between the rooms. Scheck seemed confused, as he said he'd heard Schubring walking around in the middle of the night, not the other way around. Neither had left their beds the whole night.

When Jessica and her roommate returned from their vacation, she jokingly asked if the ghost had behaved itself while they'd been away. Schubring felt dumbfounded, asking, "What ghost?" Only then did everything seem to click as the two women described their own strange experiences with the entity that haunted their apartment. Neither Scheck nor Schubring had known about the haunting prior to their stay. Scheck said that although he does believe in the paranormal, human psychology and other logical rationale can explain a situation more often than not. After his stay, he said, "What happened in that apartment I can't explain. I can convince myself of logical explanations for the voices, the cold, the feelings, but not the physical touch. Something sat on me, and it wasn't the cat."

Not too long after the vacation to New Orleans, Jessica's roommate ended up moving out. One afternoon, Jessica found herself alone in the apartment and decided to lie down on the couch for a quick nap. She had almost fallen asleep when she became aware of a rhythmic knocking sound from the wall behind her that the couch sat against. Nervous, she tried to think of a logical explanation as she lay there. She remembered the grandfather clock her father had recently purchased. It must have been sitting up against the same wall downstairs. Confidently, Jessica sat up from the couch, about to dismiss her fears, when she heard three loud bangs on the wall behind her. At first, she was frozen, but soon she found herself laughing. "Got me.…You got me," she said, a little unnerved but also amused at the situation. Jessica thought that perhaps her attitude could have been the reason that the spirits didn't seem to mess with her as often. "I respected the fact that they were here, once I accepted it, but I also wasn't afraid."

Jessica recalled one experience fondly, saying she had always worn a rose quartz point necklace while she lived there. She had a routine. Each night when she returned home, she'd place her purse, keys and necklace down on the entryway table. One morning, when Jessica came to the table, she found everything sitting there, sans one rose quartz necklace. After searching high and low, she gave up, figuring it had been the ghosts and that they would return it when they felt like it. After weeks of nothing, one morning she saw something shiny there on the table beside her keys and purse. The object in question wasn't her necklace but in fact a small silver diamond solitaire ring. She said later she even had the ring tested and was surprised to find out that it was in fact real. Jessica knew no one else had been in her apartment and believed it was a "more than fair exchange." She said she kept the ring for decades, but after one move, she lost it. "I still mourn the loss of my ghost ring but not my crystal necklace."

CHAPTER 6

THE PECK HOUSE

O n the charming brick roads of College Avenue stands a pleasant red Italianate home with a gabled roof, wide white trim and decorative brackets. The entrance to the home is through two double doors nestled between two narrow square pillars atop a petite porch, accented by dentil molding. The house has stood here since the mid-1800s and has served as a home for countless Racine residents. The first, however, was Erastus C. Peck (1837–1902).

DECADES OF HISTORY

Erastus C. Peck was born in Bristol, Connecticut, and came to Caledonia with his parents in 1841. There, he lived on their farm until 1872, when he was elected the county clerk. Before, he had served as a chairman of the Caledonia Town Board of Supervisors and was also a member of the County Board. He served as county clerk until 1874 and again from 1876 to 1886. Peck married Helen Sears (1843–1879) in 1865, and they had two children, Lillian (1867–1942) and Lewis (1864–1937). Helen passed away, having been bedridden for an extended period of time, in March 1879. Peck's mother—Sarah Peck (1798–1889)—came to live with the family to help her son raise the children and help him run his household.

In 1882, Clara Barry (unknown) sold Lot 10, Block 33 for $3,250 to Peck. This was to be the future site of his College Avenue home. In 1883, he began

The Peck House, current day, *Author's collection.*

building his residence, and the home was completed between 1884 and 1885 at a cost of $4,500. In 1886, his home was the 143rd in Racine to have the new luxury of running water from the Racine Water Department. Peck, having been county clerk, was quite familiar with abstracts and became *the* Peck of Knight and Peck Title Firm. On February 21, 1889, Peck's mother, Sarah, died in their home from a bout of pneumonia. She had been the second-oldest woman in Racine, at ninety-two years old, and had lived under the administration of every United States president up until that point. She was known as a very intelligent and cultivated woman. Her funeral was held at the home on February 23 at 2:00 p.m.

By the time his mother passed, Peck's children had already grown up, and he left his College Avenue home to live in a nearby boardinghouse on Wisconsin Avenue. While boarding, Peck rented his home out to various Racine residents until his death in 1902. In 1904, Lewis and Lillian sold their father's home to William Krantz (unknown). Krantz did not keep the house very long, and the property passed through the hands of a slew of owners until 1927, when Thomas (1868–1938) and Myrtle Sanders (1871–1941) purchased the home.

Thomas Sanders was the principal of the nearby Washington Junior High School, which was only a few blocks away. Unfortunately, in 1938, the now retired principal was struck by a car while crossing the road at Tenth and Wisconsin Streets by his home. The injuries he sustained were fatal, and he passed away at the nearby St. Luke's Hospital. Sanders had been beloved by his students and was known as the "Father of the Washington School," according to a *Journal Times* article published on November 14, 1938, the day Sanders passed. Shortly after the death of her husband, Myrtle Sanders moved out in 1939.

In 1943, attorney William Storms (1909–1973) lived there with his wife, Josephine (1907–2004). They stayed in the home until 1973. Educators seemed to be drawn to the home. From 1977 to 1987, it was occupied by teachers Carl and Susan Hipp, and from 1987 to 1998, teachers Thomas and Renee Gagliano lived there. For a brief period between 1998 and 2000, Robert and Rebecca Venn used the home for their graphic design business. In October 2000, Bob Groth and Bill Hansen purchased the home, expanding the kitchen; replacing the windows; adding a reclaimed brick patio, waterfall and koi pond into the backyard; and adding the quaint iron fence that stands out front. Their ownership is best summed up by this excerpt from the 2021 Preservation Racine Tour of Historic Homes booklet: "They have lovingly maintained and improved the property inside and out for the continued enjoyment of its owners and passers-by for years to come."

NEVER ALONE

When Groth and Hansen moved into their new home on College Avenue, they had no idea that they would soon experience some of the strangest phenomena in their lives. Hansen said that the first abnormal occurrence was the soft footsteps in the attic that would run back and forth, as if a small child was playing above them. In addition to the footsteps, a small wind-up carousel music box would go off in the middle of the night. The antique music box had been bought purely for decoration, and neither Hansen nor Groth ever wound it.

Hansen's suspicions seemed to be confirmed after a coworker of his from Western Publishing came to their home one night. The two were in the breakfast room when Hansen noticed that she kept looking over her shoulder. After a long while, she said, "You have ghosts." Hansen, though surprised, knew she was correct. The coworker asked to look around the house, and after a little while, she told Hansen that she believed the house was inhabited by the spirit of a little girl who had fallen to her death. She wasn't sure of the exact nature of the death and said that it could have been a fall from a window, staircase or perhaps the widow's walk on the house. After his coworker's visit, not much changed in the home until, while out and about, Groth and Hansen ran into the former owner of the house. The former owner had only occupied the house for eighteen months, an unusually short period. After talking with him for a while, the owner asked, "Have you had anything unusual happen?" At that point, Hansen and Groth *knew*.

After their chat with the owner, unusual occurrences seemed to escalate in the house. Hansen described on several occasions smelling pipe tobacco while they were sitting upstairs watching TV. Alarmed, he would run downstairs to see what the smell of burning could be, only to find nothing amiss. Similarly, when coming home from work and entering the breakfast room where their antique cast-iron stove sits against the back wall, he would smell fresh chocolate chip cookies. A former cleaner of the house also had smelled chocolate chip cookies in the same room while no one else was home. Other guests in the house have caught the scent of both baking cookies and bread. The stove has never been hooked up and has always been a purely decorative piece. Notably, many years later while renovating one of their upstairs rooms and adding a larger window, builders discovered a small box in the wall containing an old German newspaper clipping, a small game of checkers and a wooden French Briar tobacco pipe engraved with the initials "S.D." Hansen asked the builders to replace the box in the wall, but they kept out the tobacco pipe, which now sits in a drawer in the breakfast room.

Hansen usually worked late, and one night, while Groth was up waiting for him, he was gathering garbage from the house to put out in the driveway for garbage pickup the next morning. After gathering everything up, Groth realized he still had to go to the basement to clean the cats' litter box. Groth was not fond of heading into the basement, as it was dark and the only lights were operated by pull cords. He also had a fear of someone sneaking in through one of the old windows that did not completely lock. Groth took his dog, a Shar Pei named Toughie, and carried him down the stairs for companionship. Toughie was afraid of the basement stairs and would never go down the stairs himself due to the open backs of each step. After going through the first room and into the next, where the cat litter was located, Groth looked through another door into pitch darkness and felt uneasy. He closed that door and propped a large theater chair up against it at an angle so that while he cleaned the litter box with his back turned, nothing could come up behind him. Toughie was pacing in circles as Groth emptied the litter box, when suddenly, they were interrupted by a huge crash. From behind Groth, the heavy theater chair had fallen down onto the ground, and the door swung open. According to Groth, "That dog ran up those stairs like somebody shot him out of a cannon! And there I am, like a little schoolgirl, screaming, right behind him." Groth followed his dog up the stairs, slamming the basement door shut and locking it. He and Toughie waited outside the house in the front yard for a while until Hansen came home. Later, Hansen teased his partner about locking the basement door, as if locking a door could stop a spirit from passing through it.

In another incident, Groth was headed to grab ice cream for himself and his partner, which would lead him past the door to the attic. The men kept a flashlight on the attic door, as the attic light was hard to access—especially in the dark. The flashlight that they kept on the door had a bottom that twisted, which connected the battery to the light to turn it on, rather than an on/off switch. At the time, the neighborhood had been experiencing periodic power failures. After having passed the attic door, something made Groth feel as if he had to look back. Slowly, Groth turned and saw that the flashlight had turned on, illuminating the dim hall. Milliseconds later, the power went out. Perhaps the spirits were trying to assist him.

Another time, while lying in bed at night, Hansen felt as if someone had sat down on the edge of the bed next to him. The bed seemed to move, as if a child were sitting on the edge kicking their legs back and forth.

Hansen initially thought this could have been his cat, but when he got up to investigate, he noticed that she was asleep down the hallway. His gut sank, and he knew that something—or someone—had been on the bed beside him. To this day, Hansen tends to sleep diagonally across his bed to prevent the experience from reoccurring.

Groth has a nightly routine with his pet birds. He owns a blue-and-gold macaw and a blue-fronted amazon that both have their own large cages in their own room at the end of the upstairs hall. Each night, Groth lets them out and tends to them, then gives them a small snack and fresh food and water before putting them to bed. However, one night when he opened the door, he heard his blue-fronted amazon chirp "hello," and when Groth looked up, the bird sat atop his cage, loose in the room. The cage doors were still locked and closed. Groth couldn't believe his eyes, as he knew he had not let the bird out earlier.

The spirits in the house seem to be fond of Groth and Hansen's many animal companions throughout the years. A previous dog of theirs would sit to the left of the stove in the breakfast room and stare at the wall. While remodeling, Groth and Hansen discovered this spot had once been a doorway up to the servants' staircase. However, it remains walled off to this day. One of their previous dogs, Olivia, liked to watch TV in the upstairs room, and sometimes, while watching, her head would turn and she would look around her as if she saw something out of the corner of her eye. Rosie, their current dog, seems to experience this same thing. Sometimes, Rosie also inexplicably jumps up and runs into the hallway to sniff and investigate Groth's bedroom. Barney, their other dog, has never seemed to experience anything.

One night, after coming back from a downtown walk, Hansen entered the front door and heard the sounds of two very distinct voices coming from upstairs and getting closer, as if they were walking down the stairs. He couldn't quite make out what they were saying in the moment, but as each step creaked, it was as if he knew exactly where they were. As they came to the landing, where Hansen was in view, the voices stopped, as if the unseen entities could see him.

In a separate incident, in the evening after coming home from work, Hansen was having a cigarette in the breakfast room. The house was eerily quiet. While he was smoking, he suddenly felt a harsh, cold breeze sweep through him, as if it had come from the kitchen doorway to his left. The embers of the cigarette even extinguished for a moment, as if the breeze had disturbed them. Hansen put down his cigarette right away and tried to follow the spirit upstairs, but it seemed as if it had taken the blocked-off route up the servants' staircase, and Hansen lost the cold spot. Although Hansen couldn't see these spirits, it wouldn't be long before he did.

While bringing Olivia her supper one night, Hansen ascended the same servants' staircase. As he got to the top of the stairs, he turned to look down the hallway and saw the full-bodied apparition of a woman from behind. Her hair appeared to be in a tight gray bun, and she wore a white blouse with puffy sleeves and a full, floor-length skirt. Hansen even recalled the geometric pattern at the bottom of the skirt. To him, she looked almost like a Victorian housekeeper. Just as quickly as she appeared, she walked around the corner and disappeared, as if she had gone down the front staircase. Looking back, Hansen wondered if she was the spirit of Sarah Peck, Mr. Peck's deceased mother. After all these incidents, Groth and Hansen called in the experts.

In October 2011, the South East Wisconsin Paranormal Investigation Team (SEWPIT) came to the home to investigate. During their investigation, they held a flashlight session, in which they used a touch-sensitive flashlight—similar to the kind that was hanging on the attic door—to communicate with the spirits of the house. During the session, the investigator asked the spirit to turn the flashlight on and off at different brightness levels in accordance with their questions, and the spirits seemed to comply. The dogs were present in the room during the session and seemed to become increasingly uneasy as it went on, pacing and whining in the room. One team member asked the presence if it wanted them to move the dogs upstairs, out of the room, and in response, the flashlight turned on. The team escorted the dogs upstairs, and while they were gone, the video recording of the investigation captured the flashlight rolling around on the table on its own, continuing to turn on and off.

As they returned to the breakfast room, the team heard a loud yowling sound from the basement and quickly ran to investigate, taking the camera along with them. In the basement, Groth and Hansen's cat sat on one of the storage shelves where she had been earlier in the night but appeared distressed and continued to yowl. The team was baffled, as she appeared to be fine, and just as quickly as her wails began, they ceased. Later in the night, during a spirit box session in the first-floor living room, investigators asked the spirits if they were pleased with the renovations that Groth and Hansen had completed on the home. Both a male and female voice came from the spirit box, seconds apart, responding with a "yeah." Nearing the end of the night, and their investigation, while upstairs, SEWPIT investigators caught

EVP of disembodied whistling and a video recording of orbs coming and going from Groth's bedroom. After their investigation, they compiled their recordings onto a DVD and gave it to the couple.

Since the investigation, things have gone on as usual in the home, with the same phenomena continuing. Hansen and Groth have also had items go missing, only to reappear later in a location where neither man would have put them. For instance, Hansen's reading glasses, which are always located on the kitchen island or breakfast table, recently disappeared and have yet to reappear. Despite searching, they know the glasses are gone and will reappear in time, just like other items in the house have over the years. While staying in the guest bedroom of the home, Groth and Hansen's niece also witnessed her own glasses on the nightstand behind her shaking in the middle of the night. The couple jokes that perhaps the spirit of Mrs. Peck currently needs reading glasses to read a rather long novel—maybe *War and Peace*.

Lately, while the couple is watching TV in their upstairs living room, Groth has noticed a strange phenomenon. From his seat, he can see out into the hallway to his own bedroom door, where a lamp sits on his dresser, usually lit at night. Out of the corner of his eye, Groth can occasionally see a shadow pass in front of the reflection of the light on the woodwork, as if something had stepped in front of it and disrupted the light waves. Groth claimed that this experience had been happening more frequently as of late. It seemed similar to the phenomenon that Rosie and Olivia had also experienced.

Though their experiences have been strange and sometimes frightening, Groth and Hansen have made peace with the fact that their home is haunted. They've put significant time, energy and love into remodeling the home and preserving its historical integrity. When making any changes to the home, like their most recent remodel of the kitchen, they always ask the spirits for permission, and spiritual activity seems to temporarily rise during each change. It always settles back down again, and Groth, Hansen and their ghostly housemates live together in a strange kind of harmony.

CHAPTER 7

THE AHRENS HOUSE

Sitting in a neighborhood full of gorgeous historic homes is the Ahrens House. The home is a pale Queen Anne–style residence with tall windows, an octagonal turret, a sunny enclosed porch and a ruddy peaked roof. At the top of the turret is an old weathervane that can be seen spinning on windy days. The four-bedroom home is a whopping 2,922 square feet and features a two-story carriage house, which stands directly behind the house. The property is unique, even in a neighborhood full of so many gems. The Ahrens House has an aura of progress, as through the years it has withstood many changes and renovations to suit each owner's needs. The current owner has done a wonderful job of restoring many of the home's original features.

PALACE ON PARK AVENUE

The Ahrens House was designed and constructed by Josiah Hocking (1851–1926) in 1897 for Otto Ahrens (1855–1928) and his wife, Eleanor (1859–1898). Unfortunately, not long after moving in, Eleanor Ahrens died in her new home at only thirty-nine years of age due to complications from a tumor. In 1899, Ahrens married his new wife, Julia Deborah Currier (1873–1957), a twenty-six-year-old woman from Michigan. After bringing his bride back to Racine, however, Ahrens chose not to bring her back to

The Ahrens House, current day. *Author's collection.*

the home he had shared with Eleanor, instead opting to move into another house on the same block.

According to the 1900 city census, a young Alexander J. Horlick (1873–1950) lived in the Ahrens House with his wife, Bertha (1874–1949); baby daughter, Helen (1898–2000); and a servant and nurse, Thyra Anderson (1874–unknown) and Margarat Slesak (1876–1953), respectively. Notably, twelve years later in 1912, Horlick would commission Hocking to build the large mansion at the corner of Main and Tenth Streets locally known as the Christmas House.

In 1906, Owen Roberts (unknown) and Julius J. Cohen (unknown) are listed as living at the house together, but by 1910, the prominent Pugh family had moved in. Captain John Pugh (1847–1922) lived there with his wife, Katherine Jane Pugh (1856–1933), two sons and four daughters. In 1922, Captain Pugh passed away in his home following a short illness. The Pugh family continued to live in the home until 1947, when a news advertisement announced, "owner leaving city" and listed the home as available for occupancy within thirty days. In 1948, the Pughs sold the home to Stanley and Anna Stotkevich, who owned the property until 1955, when they sold the Ahrens home to Albert (1911–1980) and Frances (1909–1974) Schrader, who used the home as a boardinghouse, renting to gentlemen tenants. In 1960, Jakob (circa 1913–1967) and Eleanor (1920–2002) Schaeck purchased the house from the Schraders. The Schaecks continued to run the home as a rental property.

In 1964, the property was signed over from Jakob Schaeck to Eleanor, and from then on, Eleanor Schaeck was the sole owner of the property. Schaeck's tenure as a landlady was mostly uneventful, with one notable exception. In August 1969, Schaeck found one of her tenants, twenty-five-year-old Nancy A. Rich, dead inside her bedroom. After an autopsy was performed and no cause of death was determined, police declared that there was no indication of violence. After just one short mention in the August 31, 1969 *Sunday Bulletin* of the *Journal Times*, Rich's death was never again brought up.

After Schaeck's death in 2004, David Anthony and Khrystyn Nicole Carmichael owned the home from 2004 to late 2013. In 2013, Robert Shinkle Jr. owned the property for a brief time before current owners James Ratajczak and Annette Cuellar purchased the home via auction in September 2014.

The Man in the Closet

In 2006, former owner of the Ahrens house, Khrystyn Nicole Carmichael took to the website Paranormal Stories to post about her experiences in the house. She said she first noticed that doors in their home would be locked occasionally, and even using the skeleton key wouldn't open them. It was never permanent, and which doors seemed to be unable to be opened changed from time to time. After that came the noises, which although they were odd didn't seem that unusual for an old house. Shortly before they began renovation of the home, her dogs also began to act strange, always barking at a rocking chair that sat in her dining room. After she moved the chair to an upstairs bedroom, the dogs refused to go near it.

When they first started renovating their new house, the Carmichaels were sure to take lots of pictures, but for whatever reason, none of the images they took in their dining room would ever come out clearly. The images were always a little blurry and seemed to be filled with orbs. Each time Carmichael and her husband would begin a new project in the home, they started to notice faces that would appear in reflections and shadows throughout the house. Carmichael said the faces always seemed to be the same three—an older man, a child and a forlorn-looking woman.

After Cuellar moved into the home, she, too, began to notice bizarre occurrences and joked that after a while she was known as "the crazy lady who moved into the haunted house." Cuellar described her experiences in the house by saying, "At first it was kind of upsetting, which turned into obnoxious, which we now just take in stride." Cuellar said that when they found the home in the fall of 2014, they were looking for a fixer-upper and saw the Park Avenue home as the perfect opportunity. The home had gone to auction, and within a week, they were informed that they had made the winning bid and were the proud new owners of the property. Cuellar and her husband decided the best course of action would be to finish renovating their new home before moving in. Soon, Cuellar found herself setting up camp in the house, starting on the renovations during the week while her husband looked after their home in Illinois. On the weekends, the two would work on the improvements together, doing their best to make their new space livable.

Cuellar quickly settled into her weekday routine, starting work at 6:00 a.m. and finishing up by 7:00 p.m. to relax on the front porch with a cup of tea and her loyal Hungarian Vizsla, Bella, at her feet. Though Cuellar heard the occasional strange noise or two in her first weeks on the property, she wasn't unnerved, sure it was the typical "new house noises" that came with any new home. They would take some getting used to, but in no time, they'd fade into the background and become just another part of the routine.

Cuellar's first encounter occurred one night around 3:00 a.m. when she found herself tossing and turning in bed, unable to fall asleep. From outside the open master bedroom door, she heard a small noise—like someone had dropped something like a pencil in the hallway. Bella suddenly stood up on the bed and began to growl. Cuellar tried to shush her and listen, but soon Bella began to pace in circles around the bed, continuing to growl. Cuellar steeled herself and got up, peeking into the hallway, but nothing seemed to be there. She decided to do a thorough walkthrough of the house to be sure what she had heard wasn't an intruder. As she concluded her search, nearing five o'clock in the morning, she found nothing. She tried to convince herself it was nothing but still couldn't seem to get back to bed, so instead, she made herself a cup of coffee and sat on the front porch with Bella.

For another few weeks, it was business as usual in the home. Late one night, however, Bella woke Cuellar from her slumber when she started to growl into the hallway. Cuellar snapped into consciousness when Bella began to bark. Again, she found herself shakily searching the entire house. Still, there was nothing, and she was left wondering what on earth could be causing Bella's unusual behavior. Time passed, and life seemed to carry on in the home for several weeks uneventfully until Bella had another episode.

Cuellar described her dog's bark as more than her usual alert when for the third time she was woken up from sleep. This time, Bella sounded truly afraid of what was out there in the hall. From where Cuellar sat in bed, she could hear the floorboards in the hall creaking. Bella whimpered and began to pace in circles on the bed as a frightened Cuellar tried to console her. Suddenly, Bella wet the bed. Cuellar said at that moment she truly felt watched, as if someone was there with them. Upset, she searched the house, unable to find anything unusual yet again. Tired and freaked out, she found her emotions turning to annoyance. Now she would have to take all the bedding down to her house in Illinois just to wash it.

After everything that had happened, Cuellar decided perhaps a friend would take her mind off the unusual occurrences. Soon, her friend from Minnesota was on her way to spend the week with Cuellar and see her new house. Cuellar said she didn't tell her friend, Patty, about anything that had happened, reasoning that it would only make her uncomfortable. Besides, if nothing happened at all, she would have freaked out her guest for nothing. The first night Patty arrived, everything went according to plan and nothing unusual occurred. Cuellar found herself relieved and began to relax.

Cuellar's relief didn't last long when, at 2:00 a.m. on the second night, she awoke to a soft knocking at her door. It was Patty, who seemed shaken, saying that she had woken up and thought she'd seen a man standing at the foot of her bed. She scrambled to get up and turn on the light, but when she did so, no one was there. Cuellar invited Patty in, and the two slept in her bed that night with Bella cuddled between them.

The third night, after being asleep for only a few hours, Cuellar was again awoken by a knocking on her door. Patty swore she had felt someone sit down on the bed next to her. She was considerably more disturbed than the night before. Cuellar and her friend went downstairs in an attempt to take her mind off the unnerving incident. They chatted by the fireplace until late the next morning. After some breakfast, the two still felt exhausted and decided to get back to sleep. Cuellar took the guest room that time and let Patty have her room.

The fourth night, the women had both planned to sleep in their own rooms, but Cuellar knew that would not be the case when, at 1:00 a.m., Patty was knocking on her bedroom door. This time, she had awoken to see the closet door by the foot of the bed slowly creaking open, swishing across the plush carpet. Patty told Cuellar she wouldn't spend another night in the guest room and instead swapped rooms with her. This time, Cuellar let Patty keep Bella in the master bedroom with her. The following evening, the two women sat talking in front of the fireplace when the empty rocking chair beside them began to rock on its own. Patty decided that night that she would be leaving the following morning and did so, cutting her visit short by several days. To this day, Cuellar says that Patty refuses to visit her at her Racine home.

For a while after Patty's visit, not much seemed to happen in the home until Bella, again, began to act strange. Cuellar woke up to her dog whimpering, trembling and crying. She seemed to be too afraid to even bark. Cuellar said that Bella wet the bed once more but this time stayed put. "She was trembling so bad I had to wrap her in a blanket and carry her down the stairs. This was no easy feat, as she weighs 65 pounds." After calming her dog down, Cuellar said she was angry. She walked through the house shouting at the spirits, "If you want to reside here, I'm okay with that. BUT! You will NOT keep scaring my dog. If you continue to frighten my dog like this, neither of us will reside here because I will burn this house to the ground, and you'll be haunting an empty lot! DO YOU UNDERSTAND ME??!!" From that night on, Cuellar left Bella with her in-laws or daughter while finishing up renovations.

At one point, for about a year, Cuellar's friend Michele moved into the guest bedroom. Occasionally Michele would see the closet door in her room open and a gentleman walk out, around the bed and through the closed door into the hallway. She also felt the sensation of someone sitting beside her in bed and sometimes woke up to see the same man standing at the edge of her bed. Cuellar said Michele was more sensitive to the paranormal but always took it in stride, not feeling threatened by her unexplained experiences.

Cuellar's daughter also helped her with the renovations and continued to live in the house afterward, experiencing many strange incidents while inside the home. On a day when she was in the house alone, Cuellar's daughter thought she heard the sounds of multiple dogs running up the stairs and into the hallway. She guessed that her mother had come home early with her dogs, but when she checked, no one was home. Another time, she was sitting in her bedroom—the third bedroom upstairs, as she also felt too uncomfortable to sleep in the guest room—when she heard a cacophonous crash from the first floor. Cuellar's daughter rushed downstairs to find many of their baking pans, which had been securely stored on a wire shelf in the dining room, scattered across the floor. Some were as far away as four feet from the shelf.

Cuellar said the hauntings in her home seem to be most active in the fall, slowing down as winter settles in. She said her family has experienced plenty of other phantom touches, strange noises and feelings of unease throughout the house, but for the most part, the paranormal activities have faded into their everyday life.

PART III

SOUTHSIDE SANATORIUMS

The two locations covered in this section are each unique in their own right but are intrinsically linked to each other in their origins and purposes. In the early nineteenth century, the way the government treated those deemed outcasts of society was rapidly changing. The unfortunate—orphans, the poor and the physically and mentally ill—had been placed in institutions meant to separate them from and keep them out of "polite" society. Those in charge of poor farms, asylums and sanitoriums often did not have the best of intentions when it came to the care of their charges—a hardship that Isaac Taylor, the founder of the Taylor Home Orphan Asylum, experienced firsthand.

The first location, the Racine County Insane Asylum and Poor Farm, embodies this less-than-caring attitude toward its patients and charges. Overcrowding, care ranging from inadequate to abusive and general disrespect toward its residents in life and death are all hallmarks of its story. The second location, conversely, embodies the changing of attitudes as time went on. Due to his own struggles as a child abandoned to an unfit welfare system, Isaac Taylor made it his mission to found an orphanage filled with the proper love and care for children to grow and flourish. The Racine community embraced the orphanage and children rather than shun or forget about them. Though time continues to march forward, lessons learned from early American society and its attitudes can help us face our future as more informed and empathetic individuals.

CHAPTER 8

THE RACINE COUNTY INSANE ASYLUM

Located on the bustling east side of Highway 31 exists a large plot of land that currently is home to Racine's Regency Mall, the High Ridge Shopping Centre and Pritchard Park, along with several other small businesses. The site is always busy, despite many vacant storefronts. The parking lot and roads that surround the businesses have seen better days and allude to the unfortunate state of many of the unused buildings. Towering above the plaza stands the Racine water tower, a monument that has stood there since long before the site became a shopping center.

THE ASYLUM

The property that was once home to Racine County Insane Asylum sits between Highway 11, Twenty-First Street, Ohio Street and may even have extended west, past Highway 31. In December 1889, Racine's Asylum for the Chronically Insane was built. Over the years, it went through several name changes, including Gatliff Asylum, the County Hospital and High Ridge Hospital, but most Racine residents called it the Racine County Insane Asylum. Residents of the asylum included not just those who suffered from mental afflictions but also the elderly, immigrants and the poor. After having existed for only five years, the asylum burned down in an unexpected fire. All 133 patients were able to escape mostly unharmed, and most records

Racine County Insane Asylum, circa late 1800s. *Property of Racine Heritage Museum, All Rights Reserved.*

were saved by staff. Within the same year, a new building had already been erected. Also in the early 1900s, the county home—better known as the poor farm—was constructed on the property.

The poor farm and asylum were mostly self-sustaining, from growing their own food to raising livestock, making their own clothing and even maintaining their own burial grounds. Tunnels existed beneath the asylum, poor farm and cemetery for the discreet disposal of bodies. The cemetery was mostly for unclaimed deceased patients and inmates. Though originally the cemeteries for the poor farm and the asylum were kept separate, after inadequate record keeping and neglect of the grounds, the boundaries of each cemetery became less clear. Around 1910, Racine residents began to complain of the neglected condition of the burial grounds and the lack of headstones for many of the individuals. It is around this time that the cemeteries were officially merged. It is thought that occasionally patients were even exhumed and reburied in incorrect graves. Plans were made to remove the bodies after the land was bought by an outside party, but the cemetery instead was plowed over to even out the land. Finally in 1916, it was decided that the graves would be marked and new care and attention would be paid to the keeping of the grounds—which were thought to be home to over 250 bodies.

Though there aren't many official records on the living conditions of early asylum patients, in the 1940s, two cases were brought against staff

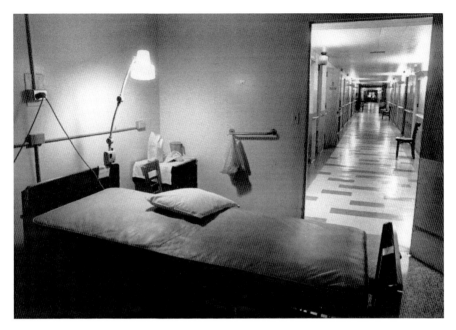

A patient's room in High Ridge Hospital, circa 1950. *Property of Racine Heritage Museum, All Rights Reserved.*

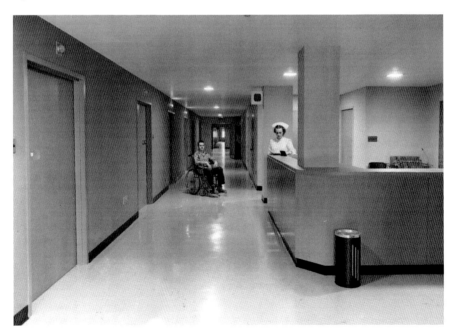

A corridor in High Ridge Hospital, 1953. *Property of Racine Heritage Museum, All Rights Reserved.*

View from the Regency Mall parking lot of High Ridge Hospital. *Property of Racine Heritage Museum, All Rights Reserved.*

members of the asylum for abuse, neglect and use of excessive force. Mr. and Mrs. Overson were employed as an orderly and a matron at the asylum, respectively. They were accused of handling patients roughly, using turpentine to make patients easier to handle and keeping female patients confined in straitjackets and straps for over twelve hours per day; in some cases, the patients had discolored hands due to lack of blood flow. In cases where restraints are misused, they can cause mental duress and physical injury including, but not limited to, stretching nerves, muscles and tendons, which can cause severe nerve damage. The court witness and expert both testified to the cruelty of these actions. However, they were unable to prove beyond a reasonable doubt that these actions could be classified as abuse.

In 1954, a visiting psychiatrist likened the facility to a medieval dungeon and criticized the care as "lacking and inadequate." Similar to the poor record keeping in their cemeteries, patient records were also incorrectly kept. In 1971, the employees of the asylum went on strike, citing the degrading treatment of patients. The asylum was closed not long after and was razed sometime in the 1980s. The pond that used to sit on the far edge of the property still remains in front of the High Ridge Centre.

Also on the property was the Sunny Rest Tuberculosis Sanitorium. Opening in November 1913, the sanitorium helped treat thousands of

An aerial view of the High Ridge Hospital campus. *Property of Racine Heritage Museum, All Rights Reserved.*

Sunny Rest Sanitorium. *Property of Racine Heritage Museum, All Rights Reserved.*

patients who suffered from tuberculosis (often referred to at the time as consumption). Though treatment was often successful, unfortunately, many patients still died from the disease while there. In 1962, the sanatorium was closed, as tuberculosis was no longer the rampant threat it had once been in Racine, thanks to the tuberculosis vaccine's widespread use.

AFTER-HOURS APPARITIONS

Employees at the High Ridge Centre's businesses have many stories to tell about the alleged paranormal activity they have experienced. At the former Kmart—which now lies vacant—the dressing room doors would slam open and shut, carts would roll around the aisles with no one pushing them and items would frequently fall off the shelves even when they appeared to be perfectly stable. Ron Helmick, founder of RPI, was employed there before the Kmart closed. He said that he personally was witness to many of the strange noises that would occur and saw things being thrown from the shelves when no one else was around. Racine residents also claim that during the construction of the Kmart, the walls inexplicably collapsed multiple times. One former employee said that she had to pick up the same fallen item multiple times in a single shift. Another former employee claimed that after her closing shift, Christmas music kept coming on over the speakers, even after they had turned everything off for the night.

A Racine resident, Johanna Fusko, said that even though she had only visited the Kmart itself a handful of times before its closing, she had sensed something off about the location. Fusko experienced what she called a "depressive state" the entire time she was in the store, and her shopping companion seemed to become uncharacteristically angry during their visits. Fusko admitted the change in their moods seemed to lift only after they had reached the far east side of the High Ridge Centre lot, near the Home Depot. On a separate occasion, Fusko was riding home with a family friend after a long night at work when they stopped at Culvers, located on the south side of the lot. While driving past the front of the empty Kmart storefront, she saw a woman inside the store, illuminated by the few security lights throughout the store and the glow of the parking lot lights. The woman was standing about ten feet back from the windows and wore a pale medical gown. However, as soon as the apparition appeared, once Fusko passed one of the vertical window frames, the woman was gone.

The High Ridge Centre, current day. *Author's collection.*

Regency Mall employees also witnessed signs that would mysteriously fall over and heard strange and unnerving sounds. Security cameras and sensors also detected movement well after the mall was closed for the night and no one was there. Some employees jokingly blamed these occurrences on "ghost children." Mall employees have also claimed to have heard wailing from the large storm drain that sits at the edge of the pond on the High Ridge Centre's property.

Behind Regency Mall, in Pritchard Park, apparitions have been spotted multiple times in wooded areas, and sometimes at night, strange sounds and voices can be heard in the woods. A group doing a paranormal investigation even caught an EVP of a disembodied voice while recording on the site. Others have said they feel like they are being watched or they see things out of the corner of their eye while at the park after dark. Many will not even enter the park after the sun has gone down.

Paranormal experiences even extend across Highway 31 into a popular Mount Pleasant strip mall and surrounding businesses. A prominent Racine medium believes that the site is a nexus of spiritual energy. A former employee of Lone Star Steakhouse recalled that early one Monday morning, while the manager was taking in a shipment alone by the bar, three steaks were suddenly thrown onto the kitchen floor. The cause of the flying meat was never determined. In another eerie instance, after an employee tragically died in a car crash, her employee number and accounts were removed from Lone Star's systems by the corporate office. Strangely, both behind the bar and in the kitchen, orders would show up with her name and employee number on them, even late at night after they had closed and no orders were being taken. The orders included random items, like steak or vodka tonic, but never included a table number. After many years of the phantom orders, corporate was contacted about the issue but had no explanation, as the deceased's employee number had been removed for several years.

Many believe that the sadness and suffering of both Racine's impoverished and ill remain connected to the site. Perhaps that is why, despite many efforts of renewal, much of Regency Mall and the High Ridge Centre remain vacant and businesses have often come and gone throughout the years.

CHAPTER 9
THE TAYLOR HOME
ORPHAN ASYLUM

Nestled within the green neighborhood streets of the village of Elmwood lies a cluster of buildings on an open, grassy field known as the Taylor Complex. Five Prairie-style brick cottages sit in a semicircle surrounding the center of the property. The entire campus feels serene. The design of the cottages flows seamlessly into the surrounding landscape. However, at the far edge of the property on Taylor Avenue stands a tall, pale monument that interrupts the level property around it. This monument alludes to the site's former purpose—the Taylor Home Orphan Asylum.

THE TAYLOR HOME'S BEGINNINGS

Isaac Taylor (circa 1807–1865), a prominent Racine businessman, had a dream. Taylor had been orphaned as a child and faced many hardships. As an adult, he was able to overcome the hardships of his youth and make a successful and comfortable life for himself and his wife, Emmerline Taylor (1815–1866). Taylor never forgot the mistreatment he had received at the hand of many of his male caretakers, and he vowed that if he ever had the means, he would create his own orphanage and protect children from the abuses he had faced as a ward of the state.

The original Taylor Home building, circa 1890. *Property of Racine Heritage Museum, All Rights Reserved.*

Another view of the original Taylor Home building, circa 1890. *Property of Racine Heritage Museum, All Rights Reserved.*

Unfortunately, in November 1865, Isaac Taylor passed away from pneumonia. Emmerline Taylor resolved to make her husband's dream a reality. Though she passed away only one year after her dear husband, in her will she created the foundations for the Taylor Home.

Thirty-eight acres of farmland south of Racine city limits were purchased to begin the orphanage. Construction began in 1868 and was not completed until 1872. On July 17, 1872—the anniversary of Mrs. Taylor's birth—the orphanage officially opened. Thanks to an endowment Mrs. Taylor had left, the orphanage was able to be self-sufficient, growing its own fruits and vegetables and raising livestock such as cows, chickens and pigs. The children's meals consisted of the fruits of their labor, and excess food was sold back to the community to sustain the continued operation of the orphanage. Though the work was hard, many orphans remember their time at the orphanage fondly.

In the years that the Taylor Home served as an orphanage, over one thousand children passed through its doors, often due to the loss of parents from war, poverty and disease—especially tuberculosis. These children were able to live the exact kind of life Isaac Taylor had hoped they would. The Racine community rallied around them and made sure the orphans enjoyed plenty of fun events and entertainment, such as ice cream socials, magic shows, fairs, concerts and open houses. Its exceptional reputation would forever be cemented in the Racine community.

In 1955, however, when the State of Wisconsin passed legislation that shut down orphanages in favor of foster care and social welfare, the fate of the Taylor Home was uncertain. However, it adapted and abandoned the orphanage model, instead focusing on becoming an institution to care for the "mentally disturbed and troubled youth"—dubbed "psychological orphans" by John Kearns, the director of the Taylor Home at the time. Kearns believed that a child "needs to understand his own negative behavior, rather than becoming resentful and trying to 'get back at society' for what he thinks life has done to him." The Taylor Home adopted Kearns's attitude and did its best to help its wards become successful adults. Throughout the 1960s, five newer cottage-style buildings gradually replaced the older Gothic-style building. The original Taylor Home building soon was used as nothing more than a dining hall. By 1973, all five cottages were complete, and the original Taylor Home building was razed.

Although most of the memories associated with the Taylor Home were positive, occasionally sadness visited. Records for the orphans and wards who lived at the Taylor Home are sealed, so we will never know how many

The Taylor Home Monument, current day. *Author's collection.*

children may have passed away while there, especially during Racine's several epidemics, including scarlet fever, influenza and tuberculosis. However, over the years, three different caretakers died while employed at the orphanage. Nellie Jane Wright (unknown–1933) came to the orphanage as a child with a limp and a crutch. Her records listed her as a "little lame girl," but her disability never held her back. The orphanage was Nellie's favorite place, and she enjoyed her time there so much that she never left, becoming a caretaker there as an adult. For sixty years, Nellie cared for and befriended the children of the Taylor Home, until 1933, when she died of a heart attack. In similar circumstances, Medora Roskilly (1890–1952), the supervisor of the Taylor Home, passed away of a heart attack in her room in 1952. Though fire and rescue squads were called, Roskilly was already dead when they arrived.

The strangest death was that of Nora Harnett (unknown–1899), although she did not die on the orphanage grounds. Nora was a well-liked and cheerful young lady, employed as a domestic servant at the orphanage. To the shock of everyone who knew her, one April day in 1899, Harnett swallowed two ounces of carbolic acid while walking down Sixth Street in downtown Racine. She left behind three letters: one to her mother, one to the orphanage and one to the gentleman who was to deliver her letters. The contents of all three letters are unknown.

Haunts of the Taylor Home

Currently, the Taylor Home is privately owned and houses various institutions, including the administration of the Village of Elmwood Park, a hall and gym space for rental purposes. Formerly, cottage number five was home to grades kindergarten through second of EverGreen Academy. The private school's higher grades were located at a different site down the road from the Taylor Complex, also on Taylor Avenue. Cottage number five, however, was often the site of many strange and unusual occurrences reported by teachers at the school during its operation.

In the lobby of cottage five sits the receptionist desk, facing the main entrance. While sitting at the desk, several staff members have heard the sounds of children running and giggling and the rustling of papers posted on the hall walls. Though there is a direct line of sight down the main hallway to the right of the desk, the hall is always empty when these sounds are heard. Also, in an incident near the lobby, a teacher happened to be working inside during recess when she heard the soft voice of a child asking, "Can I go?" The teacher was confused but assumed the child had just been left behind in the building and responded affirmatively. After several moments of silence, when she did not hear the sound of the child leaving, she looked up to see that no one was there.

One afternoon, after classes had finished for the day, one of the teachers sat in room 23, continuing to work. While working, she felt as if she was being watched—as if someone was standing in the hall outside her door. Feeling unnerved, she got up to look down the hall and see if anyone was actually there. After satisfying herself that no one was wandering the halls, she shut the door to her classroom. But after sitting back down, she heard the sounds of the paper decorations on the outside of her door rustling—as if someone was running their fingers up and down them. Then, an unusual yellowish beam of light swept beneath the door before it just as suddenly disappeared.

One of the cottages at the Taylor Complex, current day. *Author's collection.*

The teacher was so unnerved by the experience that she remained in the classroom for several more hours before leaving.

In the same classroom, room 23, the same teacher also reported that both she and her students heard knocking on the door while it was open. A student once got up to open the door, but no one was there. At the end of the day, after all of the chairs were carefully stacked onto the tables, she witnessed the chairs fly off the tables and onto the ground. This teacher is not the only one who has experienced strange things in her classroom. On a few occasions, while this teacher was on personal leave, other staff who were keeping an eye on her classroom reported hearing furniture being dragged across the room. Upon investigation, it always appeared as if nothing had been disturbed. In the same hall, outside room 23 and to the right of the reception desk, multiple witnesses have reported seeing a black and somewhat shapeless shadow darting up and down the hall.

On multiple occasions while outside, teachers have spotted a woman wearing a white blouse with a stiff, tall white collar and ruffled front, with her hair tied back in a neat and tight bun, standing in one of the front windows. She always appears to be friendly, leading some staff members to speculate that she may be the spirit of Mrs. Taylor, coming back to check on her children. One of the teachers' young sons was sitting in the back of the teacher's car outside the building with his sister when he began to make faces at the car window toward the school building. When his mother asked who he was making faces at, he said he was playing with the little boy he saw in the front window. When she turned to see who her son was talking about, there was no one in the front window of the school.

The basement of cottage five also holds its fair share of stories. While alone in one of the basement classrooms, a teacher reported a feeling of uneasiness wash over her. The uneasiness turned to "an uncontrollable sadness," and she began to cry. Though she was unsure of what had caused these strange emotions and why, the feeling lingered until she had left the property and passed the stoplights on Durand and Taylor Avenues—a quarter mile from the property—when the sadness that had come over her abruptly stopped.

In the same basement, another teacher felt something touch her back. She jolted at the feeling, and one of her students noticed, asking her, "Did it get ya?" The teacher continued to have back spasms near the area where she had felt the touch for three more weeks. In the basement storage room, the lights frequently turn on and off, and there is a general feeling of oppressiveness that has been reported by those who enter the room. Once, the door to the room slammed shut behind a staff member who was entering to gather supplies for a project. Staff has also heard the sound of water running through the plumbing in the ceiling, despite the fact that no one is in the bathrooms on the floor above.

In a basement classroom, room 222, a teacher was preparing for class when she began to hear the door handle rattling from the inside of the open door. She looked up to find the doorknob still and brushed off the experience as her imagination. However, after several minutes, she heard a different doorknob rattling from across the hall, outside the room. Upon inspection, she found that a door that had been closed when she arrived was now sitting wide open. Suddenly, it slammed shut.

After all of these unsettling experiences, the Paranormal Investigators of Milwaukee came to the site in 2018 for an investigation. Throughout the investigation, many minor incidents occurred, but the team was able to come up with plausible and non-paranormal explanations for most of them. However, there are a few occurrences that stood out. The team captured an EVP recording of a soft female voice whispering something indistinct, as well as a chair shifting, in or near room 23. A teacher who came along on the investigation also felt three short breaths hit her face while sitting in the basement classroom. Nearing midnight, in the second basement classroom, the investigation was interrupted by a loud thud that came from upstairs, a sound similar to that of a large textbook being dropped in the middle of the floor or a desk being overturned. Though the team quickly made their way upstairs, the source of the noise was never determined, and nothing appeared to have been disturbed. This investigation ended early after a sudden and unexpected storm began to roll in. Despite the early end to the investigation, it seemed clear that something odd was going on in cottage five.

Racine Paranormal Investigators have also done their own investigations of the Taylor Home buildings. While in the basement of one of the cottages, investigators were going from room to room to assess the energy in each. Psychic Michael Sorensen said that while in the basement, he saw several small children come into one of the rooms, seeming curious about the team. One of the little girls went up to Doug—another investigator—and gave his leg a hug. Doug even said he felt something on his leg at the same time that Sorensen was seeing it happen. While there, they also saw a shadow man and heard a sound that Ron Helmick, founder of RPI, described as sounding like a Fisher-Price corn popper push toy. While out in the yard, one of the investigators became overwhelmed by the energy of the site and collapsed into the grass. She said she felt like someone was pushing down on her chest, and it took multiple members to pull her back up, as if something was trying to hold her to the ground.

Despite the many strange paranormal occurrences on its ground, the Taylor Home holds a special place in the Racine community. In 2015, while walking the grounds, Wendy Spencer—a well-known member of the Racine community—found a large marble slab cracked in two lying facedown where the original orphanage building had once stood. The plaque turned out to be one that had adorned the building before its demolition in 1973. With the help of the community, Spencer was able to raise funds to create a monument to the old Taylor Home Orphan Asylum. The marble slab now stands as the centerpiece of the towering monument at the far end of the property, surrounded by some of the original Cream City bricks used to construct the orphanage.

PART IV

OTHER FRIGHTS
OF RACINE COUNTY

Racine County is a vast community, rich in history and lore. The city itself, however, is not the only place ghosts are said to dwell. Somber spirits wander long stretches of road, historic buildings, wooded forests and quiet burial grounds in various towns and villages around the area. The next chapters are only two of the many fascinating paranormal locations Racine County has to offer.

CHAPTER 10

CHANCES FOOD & SPIRITS

Back in the days before Wisconsin was a state, when most of the territory was covered by vast wilderness, some adventurous men sought to settle near the Fox River and make the land their own. One such man was Levi Godfrey. Godfrey created the first tavern in western Racine County, which would become the township of Rochester. The tavern still stands—a staple on the small town's Main Street. The brick building has stood for as long as anyone alive can remember. It is constructed of the pale yellow brick that is well known in architecture throughout southeastern Wisconsin. The sturdy-looking building is not ornate, but its historic beauty is still apparent. Twelve windows adorn the front of the first two floors, which afford a wonderful view of the small downtown area.

THE UNION HOUSE

In 1836, Levi Godfrey (1810–1890) and John Wade (1803–1851) made their way into the Wisconsin territory to stake claim on a plot of land near the Fox River. When Godfrey arrived, he built the first structure in Rochester, a small log shanty that was soon added onto, becoming the first tavern in the area. Due to its prime location on the route between Milwaukee and Chicago—especially between Racine and the Mississippi River—the location was chosen as the venue for Wisconsin's first political convention, known as "Godfrey's Convention." The convention hosted many of Wisconsin's pioneers, including the founder of the city of Racine himself, Captain Gilbert Knapp (1798–1887). Travelers, too, would stop at the tavern and sleep overnight on its humble dirt floor.

In 1843, the original log structure of the building burned to the ground and was said to have been the work of the upset local Indigenous people who lived in the area. Godfrey sold the property to Peter Campbell (1804–1856). Campbell rebuilt the property in brick, with eighteen-inch-thick walls that featured small holes in the side, which were to be used to point guns out of in case the need to defend the building from another attack arose. This became the Union House building. At that time, the Janesville plank road and the U.S. Territorial Road—currently known as Highway 20—both passed near Campbell's tavern, keeping business steady through the years. In the 1850s, the Union House ceased its operations as a hotel but continued on as a tavern and also continued to host community gatherings and celebrations for the town of Rochester. It is even rumored that before the Civil War, the building may have been a stop on the Underground Railroad. Beneath the old building exist tunnels that are now blocked off by plumbing and have since been filled in but could be evidence of escape routes taken by enslaved African Americans passing through the station. This seems likely, given the strong abolitionist history in the area.

In 1856, Campbell hosted his much-anticipated July Fourth Ball. He used this occasion to dedicate his new ballroom, which was complete with a state-of-the-art springboard dance floor that still exists on the second floor of the tavern to this day. The party was so successful that Campbell was able to pay off all his debts. Unfortunately, the businessman was unable to enjoy it, as he died only three short weeks later from illness.

The ownership of the building was passed on, and it continued to operate, hosting many parties, including a notable dance in March 1921. According to the *Burlington Free Press*, the entire building was to be raffled off at the dance. Patrons could purchase a chance to own the Union House for the small fee of just $1 per raffle ticket. At the time, Mark S. Smith (unknown) owned the building, which was valued at $12,000. The winner of the raffle received the hotel on June 10, 1921. Strangely, from June 1921 through April 1923, the building remained vacant, according to records. In 1923, the building was purchased by a gentleman from Milwaukee.

Several owners came and went, until in 1956, Bill (1919–1969) and Dorothy Thiede (1915–2003) purchased the property, and it became Godfrey's Tavern, a nod to its original owner. It remained with the Thiedes

Chances Pub & Eatery, current day. *Author's collection.*

until 1987, when Tom and Debbie Schuerman took ownership and renamed their new business Chances Food & Spirits. The restaurant got its name because when the Schuermans bought it, Tom Schuerman said, "I just thought I was taking a lot of them. That's how the name stuck." To this day, the restaurant remains with Tom Schuerman and his family. His daughter Sarah Coots and sister Sue Splan manage the restaurant together. Chances continues to be a community staple in the small town of Rochester.

CHANCE ENCOUNTERS

When Tom Schuerman first purchased Chances, he didn't know that the building was rumored to be haunted. Even if he had, Schuerman confessed that he wouldn't have believed it until he had experienced it for himself. In fact, one of the first employees he hired had a husband whose family had once owned the building. She shared the stories she had heard from him and his family with then owners Tom and Debbie Schuerman. The ghosts, of which there are seven in total, include Sadie, a former cook; a set of twins believed to be between ten and twelve years old; a Civil War soldier and his long-lost love, a woman in a green gown; a young woman in a blue polka-dotted dress; and Mitch, the least friendly of the spirits. Mediums told the owners that the spirits of the location seemed to react most to strong emotions. For instance, when employees or patrons experience strong emotions, activity in the building seems to pick up.

The first spirit that former co-owner Debbie Schuerman encountered was that of a cook who haunted the kitchen and basement. She had learned from previous owners that it was believed to be the ghost of a formerly enslaved African American woman who had escaped to freedom and avoided capture by living in the basement of the Union House and working there as a cook. Because the ghost had no name, Debbie decided to call her Sadie. Sometimes stove burners will be shut off while the staff is cooking, food vanishes and the basement door in the kitchen will swing open when no one is around. A couple of former chefs at the restaurant would change into their uniforms in the back bathroom, and on a few occasions, Debbie Schuerman witnessed them running out of the bathroom, clothing still in hand, claiming that they had been touched by an unseen hand. Sarah Coots, the Schuermans' daughter, said that when a group of mediums came to dine in the restaurant, one of them alerted her to a spirit that seemed to follow her like a shadow, looking after her while she was in the building. Coots told the medium that she believed it was Sadie, to which the medium responded, "That's her slave name," which aligned with what they knew about her past. Coots said that she always felt Sadie's presence looking after her, even when she was just a toddler when her parents first bought the place. To this day, when Coots leaves for the night, she always makes sure to wish Sadie goodnight.

Sadie is thought to also be close to the twin children who haunt Chances, and when small things like silverware and cleaning supplies go missing, they can often be found in the basement. Employees believe that it might be Sadie and the twins in cahoots, enjoying a bit of mischief. Not much is known about the twins, and their presence has only ever been confirmed by a painting done by a local psychic of Chances. In the foreground of the image, two small children—a boy and a girl—are seen playing with a wagon. The painting was given to Tom Schuerman as a gift and hangs in the front of the restaurant. They believe the twins are happy, enjoying their small pranks.

The next spirit was encountered by Stacy Kopchinski, another of the Schuermans' daughters. One morning before opening, she came in to vacuum the dining room. Nothing out of the ordinary occurred until Kopchinski had finished and turned around to notice a man in a long wool coat and wide-brimmed hat sitting at the bar. She quickly grabbed a fork from one of the dining tables to defend herself with, afraid that the man was an intruder and had broken in while she was cleaning, but as quickly as he seemed to appear, he was gone. Kopchinski was shaken but also glad the gentleman had been a non-corporeal visitor rather than an actual intruder. This spirit is known as the Civil War soldier and has also been seen by some of the previous cleaning women, who would come in to clean the restaurant in the morning. However, those who have encountered the phantom have promptly quit.

Local legend has it that the soldier and another spirit, a woman in a green gown who haunts the upper floor, actually share a link to each other. Supposedly, when Chances was still known as the Union House, the lady in green was a local prostitute with whom the soldier fell madly in love. Distraught and believing herself unworthy of his love, she is said to have committed suicide upstairs. The soldier was heartbroken and took his own life on the lower level. Unfortunately, their paths never crossed in the afterlife, and the two are said to wander separate spectral planes looking for each other. Kopchinski has seen the woman in green on a few occasions. She is pale and blonde and stares out from one of the windows on the second story. Sometimes, when she drives by at night, Kopchinski can see her. Customers have occasionally asked who is living upstairs after seeing the woman in the window.

Steve Albright, a late local historian and former resident of the apartment above Chances, once heard inexplicable harp music while at home. When he went to investigate, he saw the woman in green standing at the far edge of the dance floor. Frightened, he quickly ran downstairs. This was not the only time this incident occurred, and after a few occurrences, Albright decided that he wouldn't run the next time it happened and instead stood at the top of the staircase to the ballroom and stared the spirit down. She then floated straight through him, leaving him frigid and cold, and apparently a strange and unpleasant scent lingered behind where she had just been. Others have also heard disembodied music, muffled chatter, the sounds of a woman walking across the springboard floor in high heels and someone walking up and down the stairs to the ballroom when no one is there. It is believed that the lady in green may also be responsible for occasionally knocking over chairs that are set up in the ballroom.

The other lady of Chances is a young woman in a blue polka dot dress who seems to wander the first floor. Not much is known about her, but she has been seen by waitresses walking through the dining room and into the kitchen, only to disappear. She has also been seen by Coots's four-year-old daughter, who told her mom, "Mom, the ghosts here are nothing like Casper.

They have legs, you know!" Late at night, after the lights have been turned off in the dining room, the doors to the kitchen swing open when no one is there, leading the owners to believe it might also be the woman in blue.

The final spirit is known to be ill-tempered and perhaps misogynistic. He is known as Mitch and occupies the second floor, usually staying in the apartment. Mitch was first seen by Schuerman when he had gone upstairs to turn out some of the spotlights that illuminate the gargoyles on the outside of the building. As Schuerman passed through the empty apartment kitchen, he glanced at the mirror above the sink and—according to a passage in *Haunted Wisconsin*—"saw an older, bearded, dark-haired man's face staring back at him. The outside lights have remained on since then." To avoid irritating Mitch, when employees need to go upstairs, they always make sure to let him know it is just a temporary intrusion and they will be out shortly. During a paranormal investigation, investigators asked the spirits upstairs, "Are you happy here?" Upon playback of the audio, they heard a deep masculine voice growl, "Get out" in response.

Debbie Schuerman has had quite a few interesting experiences with the spirits of Chances. One of the most annoying occurrences was the frequent disappearance of her high heels. Often, she would wear her heels to work and bring flats with her so that she could change into them as the night went on. When her feet were tired, she would place her heels in the back storage room, but when she returned, the shoes would be gone. Debbie Schuerman even tried hiding her shoes, but still, they would disappear. In *Haunted Wisconsin*, she was quoted as saying, "I think I lost half a dozen pairs of heels before I finally decided I wasn't going to wear high heels anymore." The owners have also had chairs pulled away from dining tables when no one is in the main dining area, and the heavy barstools also randomly fall over when no one is near them.

Despite the annoyances, the Schuermans have always believed that the majority of spirits at Chances are looking out for them. Debbie Schuerman once recounted an instance in which they ran out of carbon dioxide gas at the bar, which was used to pressurize the taps. The tanks of gas that supplied them were located in the basement. Since she was unsettled by venturing into the basement at night, one of her regulars accompanied her to the cellar. While she was exchanging the tanks, Debbie heard a hissing noise above her head and immediately ducked, trying to back out of the area. At first, she thought it could have been a snake, and due to her fear of snakes, she was reluctant to look up. But when she did, she noticed a leak from the ceiling below the kitchen. The leak had trickled down onto one of the basement light

Painting inside Chances, artist unknown. *Author's collection.*

fixtures and shattered the bulb. However, the filaments were still glowing; the hissing noise was caused by the water leaking down into the live electrical wire. After the tank was changed, one of the customers—who was a volunteer firefighter—assisted Debbie Schuerman in cutting power to the light fixture and capping the wire. While completing the fix, they noticed that the porcelain on the fixture and the floorboards above it had blackened due to the intense heat. The following day, the company that maintained the carbon dioxide tanks stopped by to pick up the empty one. When the employee did, however, he realized that the tank was still half full and pressurized—nothing appeared to be wrong. This led Debbie to think that the spirits had used the malfunction to warn her of the fire hazard in the basement.

Perhaps one of the most notable events to occur on Chances property was prompted by a late-night phone call Debbie Schuerman received, alerting her that one of the motion detectors had gone off inside the restaurant. She arrived at the business and went inside with sheriff's deputies, who had arrived to respond to the alarm. Together, they found no intruders but instead discovered a small leak in the hallway ceiling. A new roof had just been installed, but it seemed that the workers hadn't properly covered the seam between the newer and older sections of the restaurant. The leak was dangerously close to a light fixture. Much like the previous incident with the basement leak, she quickly shut off the power to the light to negate the fire risk. When she left the restaurant, she called out, "Thank you! I'll catch you in the morning. Keep an eye on the place!" leaving the confused sheriff's deputies to wonder who she was talking to at the time.

Customers have also experienced the hauntings, witnessing bathroom faucets turning on and toilets flushing inexplicably in the restrooms at Chances. None of the plumbing is automatic. A regular customer who once experienced this phenomenon, along with the door slamming on her, still refuses to use the bathroom at Chances to this day. Coots and her aunt Sue Splan decided to have a sleepover one night to investigate the hauntings for themselves. While they were sitting downstairs at the bar, the jukebox that they were listening to started to get louder and louder, even though no one was near the only remote. The two women freaked out as the volume increased and tried their best to turn it down, but nothing seemed to work. Suddenly, there was a loud *FWUMP*, and the jukebox powered off. After their experience, Coots and Splan decided to retire for the night, albeit a restless one. Coots joked that they had gone looking for an experience and had certainly gotten one.

Professional investigators have also visited Chances. While doing an investigation in February 2010, the Anomaly Investigation Research (AIR) investigators recorded many unexplained taps, knocks and bangs that seemed to be in response to questions investigators asked throughout the night. While downstairs, AIR also recorded EVP of a man's disembodied voice in the dining area. However, most of his dialogue was indistinguishable. Some also experienced feelings of unease and nausea, in addition to goosebumps, while standing in the hall near the coat room.

Upstairs, in the back of the apartment, AIR investigators observed strange temperature fluctuations near the apartment door, and one saw a strange humanoid shadow pass across the back wall. The ballroom was the most active location throughout the night. EMF (electromagnetic field) readings in excess of 100 milligauss were recorded by the door on the west side of the ballroom. During a spirit box session, investigators heard the box say, "Remember?" as well as a woman's voice saying, "Hi, wait there." During this session, they also captured EVP of someone walking up and down the stairs to the ballroom, disembodied chatter, soft music accompanied by a woman humming, erratic breathing, unintelligible mumbling and even a growling noise.

Haunts at Chances haven't slowed down over the years. If you ask staff about the large clock on the dining room wall, you'll find that it is the third clock to grace the position. Each time the owners try to hang a clock in the spot, it is knocked off the wall by an unseen force. Once, Splan and Schuerman were both in the dining room when the clock shot off the wall, almost six feet away, and knocked into a nearby partition. More recently, while Coots was working in the back office, she heard a loud bang, as if someone had dropped something heavy—like a large ream of paper—onto the bar. When she came out to investigate, no one was in the restaurant and nothing was out of place. Upon review of the security camera footage, the noise was audible on the recording, but nothing seemed to cause it in the frame. On Monday, December 13, 2021, Splan and Coots were both alone in the restaurant. All morning, Coots had been hearing strange sounds, like things falling off shelves and strange knocking noises. Each time she went to check for the cause of the sounds, nothing seemed amiss. Later in the afternoon, Splan and Coots were at the bar when, out of nowhere, a quarter appeared midair—about eye level—and fell onto the bar counter. The entire incident was caught on the bar's security cameras. The origin of the falling quarter still perplexes them to this day.

Recently, the owners have also been noticing the deadbolt to the front door being thrown open so that the door will be unable to shut all the way. The deadbolt cannot be turned without a key. It seems to happen both in the middle of the day and at night and both while customers are present and when the staff is alone. Perhaps notable to mention, while the author was interviewing Schuerman and Coots at the restaurant, Splan arrived, and inexplicably, the bottom of her travel mug cracked and spilled coffee all over.

CHAPTER 11

BURLINGTON CEMETERY

Along Browns Lake Drive in Burlington, Wisconsin, sits a twenty-five-acre plot of land, peaceful and green and a mere stone's throw away from Browns Lake itself. This scenic location is home to Burlington Cemetery, the city of Burlington's only nondenominational cemetery and the home to over nine thousand burial sites. The Burlington Cemetery that is visible from the road is not the only burial ground either; tucked behind trees and uphill from the main site is a gem in which many of Burlington's pioneers were laid to rest—the Old Burlington Cemetery. Both locations are cared for by the historic Burlington Cemetery Association, and both are rumored to be haunted.

TALE OF TWO CEMETERIES

The city of Burlington is located between the Fox and White Rivers, about a forty-minute drive southwest of the city of Racine. Interestingly, the city itself straddles both Racine and Walworth Counties. Burlington was first settled in 1835, and in 1848, a plank road was built, connecting the industrial and agrarian community to the city of Racine. Similarly to Rochester, a railroad quickly followed and replaced the plank road as the main means of travel to the town. In the first quarter of the twentieth century, Burlington saw a boost in population and, consequently, the construction of many new notable sites, such as a city hall, hospital, public park and—significant to this location—the chapel that currently stands on Burlington Cemetery grounds.

The land the main cemetery resides on began to be used as a burial ground for several local families in the 1840s but was owned by Burlington resident Nelson R. Norton. In 1851, Norton deeded his land to the then town of Burlington, and it became the community's first public cemetery. Throughout the years, the size of the cemetery steadily increased, and in 1911, the Burlington Cemetery Association was formed to take over ownership and care of the site. The chapel, too, is cared for by the association. The chapel, which is located on the far south end of the property, achieved recognition in the National Register of Historic Places in 2013 for its unique architecture.

Construction on the chapel began in the fall of 1921 and was completed sometime after the spring of the following year. It is constructed in a late Victorian style known as Richardson Romanesque, which gives it a somewhat ancient castle-like aesthetic. The style was most popular in the late nineteenth and early twentieth centuries, making the erection of the chapel at the tail end of this architectural fad. What makes the Richardsonian style unique from other Roman Revival architecture is its use of large round arches and monochromatic heavy stone walls. The elements of Burlington Cemetery's own chapel were described in the National Register's form as having "solid volume and simple form, weighty mass and rough-faced masonry construction, round arch, and gable parapets." The architect and builders of the chapel are both unknown.

Also according to the form, its designation as a historic location in 2013 was part of the Burlington Cemetery Association's plan to "open opportunities for financial support" to restore the chapel. Their efforts succeeded, and in 2020, work began on restoring the old chapel, starting first with its unique roof, constructed of green glazed terra-cotta tiles made by Ludowici of Chicago. On November 13, 2021, the Burlington Cemetery Association celebrated the completion of the restorative work on the chapel, which stands proudly on the southern edge of property to this day.

The Old Burlington Cemetery, which is located on the east end of the property uphill and across a grassy field, was allegedly built atop a Native American burial mound and beside an old farmhouse. This cemetery was in use from 1814 to 1927, meaning both cemeteries were in use simultaneously for a while. Don Reed, a journalist for the *Journal Times*, described the old cemetery best as "nestled on a quiet hill beneath giant red and white oak trees."

Old Burlington Cemetery, current day. *Author's collection.*

This tranquil site is known as the final resting place of many of Burlington's earliest settlers, including Albert Brown (1823–1843), a member of the Brown family that nearby Browns Lake is named after, and Origen Perkins (1801–1853), the namesake of Burlington's Origen Street. Another notable burial is that of Caroline Potter (1845–1850), whose father was the renowned John F. "Bowie Knife" Potter (1817–1899). According to legend, "Bowie Knife" Potter got his nickname while serving as a Wisconsin congressman. Not long before the onset of the Civil War, while in a contentious debate with a southern congressman, Potter was challenged to a duel. He was given the choice of weapons to be used and the location to duel at. However, after Potter made his choices known—bowie knives and a dark room—the southern congressman quickly withdrew his challenge.

Throughout the years, the Old Burlington Cemetery has fallen in and out of disrepair, being accused of becoming a "forgotten" burial ground as early as the 1940s. To make maintenance and visitation easier, a gravel road was added in 1942, linking the old cemetery with the newer main cemetery. In the modern day, the path is no longer gravel but cuts across a grassy field beside Burlington Cemetery. The Burlington Cemetery Association works hard to keep both sites maintained with the help of local community supporters. Tombstones in the old cemetery are often uncovered, repaired and reset as the site continues to receive more regular maintenance than in past decades.

Unfortunately, Burlington Cemetery Association's funds have dwindled, due in large part to an embezzlement case that began in the mid-1980s. The vice president of a local bank embezzled at least $185,000 from the cemetery association's funds, which were meant to go toward the maintenance and upkeep of the property. As costs rise, keeping up both the historic and main cemetery has become increasingly difficult. This has left the fate of both locations uncertain. Sale to a private owner or having the City of Burlington take over care of the property have both been discussed, but as of the writing of this chapter, no solution has yet been decided on. Currently, the Burlington Cemetery Association continues to accept donations toward their efforts through their website, burlingtoncemeterywi.com.

OTHERWORLDLY ENTITIES

In her book *Haunted Burlington, Wisconsin*, local author Mary Sutherland discusses some of the alleged paranormal activity at the site, the majority of which seems to come from the old cemetery. She mentions the absence of some grave markers as a possible reason why the spirits seem to be so active at the site. People who have entered both cemeteries have reported a sense that they were being watched or followed, and some even claim to have been chased from the grounds by something they couldn't see. A large black dog with piercing red eyes, believed to be a hellhound, has also been spotted at the old cemetery. It is said to have the ability to appear and disappear at will. Full-bodied apparitions standing beside their tombstones and strange white mists oozing from the grave markers have reportedly been photographed by visitors as well.

Some of this paranormal activity is discussed by a group of young friends in their visits to Burlington's cemeteries, recorded and uploaded to YouTube in June 2008. Katie, one of the explorers, expressed a feeling of extreme paranoia and anger upon crossing the threshold of the site and later in the night said she felt as if she had been shoved from behind. Katie described the push as so forceful that it felt like "something went through my chest and my heart was going to go out." In another documented visit, C.J., Katie and two other friends caught dozens of photographs of numerous orbs floating above and around the tombstones, with some even hovering in the trees. C.J. even claimed to have caught an image of two apparitions standing beside their tombstones—perhaps the photograph Sutherland mentioned in her book. C.J. spoke about the rumors they had heard about the site, including a possible vortex, sighting of orbs and a watching pair of red eyes.

In more recent years, paranormal investigation and urbex group MW Desperados have made numerous visits to the sites—both on and off camera—to investigate the alleged paranormal activity. Three of their visits are documented in uploads on their YouTube channel, also called MW Desperados. During their first video investigation, team members Mike and Abigail returned to the site due to footage they had previously recorded inexplicably corrupting after leaving the site. Using a spirit box application called Necrophonic, Abigail and Mike used the Estes Method to communicate with the spirits, setting up their base at the old chapel. The Estes Method involves one participant asking the spirits questions while another participant who is unable to see the first participant wears headphones connected to a spirit box and repeats aloud any responses they hear. During the session, the responses were initially short and somewhat hostile, but some more complete phrases came through, including, "I can't protect you" and "Am I dead?" After the session, during their walk down the cemetery paths, the Necrophonic app said, "portal," "guardian" and "tunnel," perhaps hinting at the vortex that is rumored to be located in the cemetery. During this visit, more of their footage was lost due to corruption, although the majority of it was intact.

In their second trip to Burlington Cemetery on YouTube, MW Desperados Mike and Matt headed back to see if they could find out more information on the guardian and portal previously mentioned. During the visit, investigators used the Necrophonic app to communicate with the spirits as they moved throughout the cemetery. Some of the first words that came through were "convicted," "sentenced" and "jail." All seemed too closely related to be a coincidence. While they were exploring further into the cemetery, spirit activity seemed to increase and the Necrophonic app spoke out more frequently, although none of Mike's or Matt's questions about the portal or guardian were answered. At several points during the video, both men seemed to pause and look at their surroundings, having heard branches break or the sound of footsteps shuffling through the grass around them. Each time there appears to be nothing that could have caused the sounds.

The Necrophonic app communicated several complete phrases, including "have memories," "I'm at peace" and "tell my story." The two also used a K2 meter that they had brought along—a device used to detect changes in nearby electromagnetic (EMF) fields, thought to be able to detect EMF changes that spirits might cause when nearby. While Matt and Mike were discussing these communications, the K2 meter that Mike was holding jumped up to orange—the second-highest level—and both men heard footsteps nearby. At the same time, the Necrophonic app said, "avoid this area." Not long after, the app continued, saying, "it's scary here," which prompted the K2 meter to jump up and down a few more times. The spirits continued to communicate, seeming to urge the two investigators to "share my message." Again, the meter spiked before "I was killed" came through. The investigators then said that they felt as if something "rushed them," both having heard rapidly approaching footsteps. Matt can be seen on camera taking a quick and surprised step back, as if avoiding an unseen force.

Later on in their investigation, Matt was left alone with the Necrophonic app while Mike continued to explore the grounds. The app said, "we will touch you," and at the same time, Matt thought he saw a flash of brightness in the distance among the tombstones. After he returned, Mike confirmed that the flash could not have been from him, as he had been exploring in another area with his flashlight pointed in a different direction. At one point, Mike also thought he had seen a white shape walking through the tombstones ahead of them. When they went to investigate the area where Mike had seen the shape, there was no trace of anyone or anything nearby. Nearing the end of their investigation, the cemetery began to get warmer, and the wind died down. Mike said that he thought the energy had shifted. After hearing footsteps approach the pair again, Mike and Matt heard the spirit box say, "get out." MW Desperados chose to end their investigation at this point.

In MW Desperados' final investigation, titled "Burlington Cemetery Final Chapter," team members Matt and Mike again return to the cemetery. The two discussed that this would be their final visit for some time, as spiritual energy seemed to have left the site. They talked about having had more intense paranormal experiences in their off-camera visits during the summer of 2022 and that the energy in the cemetery would shift noticeably after dark. While exploring in the old cemetery, Mike and Matt noticed that the foundation of the old farmhouse beside the cemetery was now missing and had been replaced by the construction of a new home.

They speculated that perhaps the paranormal energy had been tied to the old farmhouse foundation.

While discussing his team's visits to Burlington Cemetery, Mike again mentioned the old farmhouse's foundation and how he believed it was linked to the disappearance of paranormal activity at the site. He said that Mary Sutherland had also theorized that the farmhouse had belonged to the family plot and was also linked to the old cemetery's spirits. Mike said that their investigations in Burlington seemed to be connected to a "paranormal triangle" of locations—a phenomenon similar to the paranormal triangle of Whitewater. Making up each point of the triangle had been the Burlington Cemetery, the Old Burlington Water Tower and the Haunted Woods. Mike ended by sharing a story about two odd incidents that occurred during his visits to the cemetery.

> *Last summer, right around the end of August, I was leaving a friend's house that lived right behind the cemetery. I was walking down the road to my [car], and I heard something call my name. I looked to my left, and this thing had to be about eight feet tall, following and growling at me from the other side of the fence.*
>
> *About two years ago, Matt and I took a group up to the old cemetery part, and we were doing a Necrophonic session and the spirit was being very racially obnoxious. We had an interracial couple with us, and the spirit did not like that at all, but being an 1800s spirit from the information we gathered, that could explain the hostility. All of a sudden, we felt surrounded and pushed out of the old cemetery. Matt turned around as we were walking away and see [sic] a white mist following us to the edge of the old cemetery.*

It is strange that a location so well known for its otherworldly energy has seemingly become un-haunted. In all my research, this is the first location I have come across where the paranormal energy has lessened or ceased to exist. Perhaps both the old and new Burlington Cemetery's fates are intertwined with the uncertainty of the site's future. Without careful preservation and care, any historic site can fall victim to progress and be forgotten. Maintaining this site has been a struggle but remains important. The places where we as a society choose to bury our dead are meant to hold significance and a sense of sacredness. I hope that Burlington Cemetery can continue to persevere through these difficult times and remain an important part of the Burlington community for many years to come—ghosts or no ghosts.

Other Reportedly Haunted Locations

Downtown Sites

The Brickhouse
Carriage House Liquor Co.
The Journal Times Building
Memorial Hall
The Monument Square Building
Sheepish
The Void, formerly McAuliffe's On the Square

Lakefront Sites

The Christmas House
The S.C. Johnson Building, formerly the old St. Mary's Hospital
The VFW and Foxhole Lounge

SOUTHSIDE SITES

Elmwood Plaza
Majestic/Uptown Theater
Microtel Inn and Suites

NORTHSIDE SITES

The Racine Zoological Gardens
The Wind Point Lighthouse

CENTRAL SITES

The Midwest Market, formerly the Rapids Drive Pick 'N Save
Mound Cemetery
Racine Country Club
RAM's Charles A. Wustum Museum of Fine Arts
West Lawn Memorial Park

COUNTY SITES

Art's Town Tap
Burlington Kmart
Burlington Water Tower
Burlington Woods
Enve Salon and Day Spa
Root River Bridge on Highway 31 near the intersection with 4 Mile Road

BIBLIOGRAPHY

Chapter 1

Blattner, James F. "Racine Couple Feels Downtown Living Only Way to Go." *Journal Times*, December 21, 1975.

Burke, Michael. "Historic Downtown Building Gets Attention." *Journal Times*, March 29, 2017.

———. "New Life Vowed for Historic Downtown Building." *Journal Times*, December 15, 2016.

Current, Annabelle. "Down Memory Lane: Red Cross Drug Co." *Shoreline Leader*, June 8, 1978.

Foreman, Suzanne. "The Old Stone Building." *Preservation Racine Newsletter* 4 (Winter 1988): 9.

Givens, Billy, medium, Spiritually Charmed. In discussion with the author, November 21, 2022.

Kubik, Rachel. "That's the Spirit: Racine Paranormal Investigators Visit Social on Sixth, Seek More Haunted Locations." *Journal Times*, May 5, 2021.

Journal Times. "Remembers Opera Fire 65 Years Ago Today." December 28, 1949.

———. "Remodeled Red Cross Drug Store." March 18, 1960.

National Police Gazette. "Death in the Flames." January 17, 1885.

Pfarr, Jada, owner, Longshot Vinyl. W-mail correspondence with the author, July 2021.

Racine County Historical Museum. "A Night to Remember." *Retrospect: Racine County History Retold* 1, no. 2 (n.d.).

Racine Daily Journal. "Removing the Ruins." January 2, 1885.

———. "Weird Wreck." December 30, 1884.

Rintz, Don. "The Blake Opera House." *Preservation Racine Newsletter* 4 (Winter 1982): 2–3.

Roehre, Joan, owner, Social on Sixth. In discussion with the author, June 14, 2021.

Sharma-Jensen, Geeta. "Hills Want to Restore Old Red Cross Drug Building." *Journal Times*, January 21, 1988.

———. "Renovator Plans Diverse Uses for Historic Building." *Journal Times*, August 19, 1988.

Vertical Index. Folder 189 Fires (General). Racine Heritage Museum Archives, Racine WI.

Vertical Index. Folder 250 Red Cross Drug Company. Racine Heritage Museum Archives, Racine, WI.

Vertical Index. Folder 656.01 6th Street. Racine Heritage Museum Archives, Racine, WI.

Chapter 2

Burke, Michael. "At Ivanhoe, Things Go Bump in the Night." *Journal Times*. October 16, 2011.

Givens, Billy, medium, Spiritually Charmed. In discussion with the author, November 21, 2022.

Jones, Stephanie. "The Haunted History of Downtown Racine." *Journal Times*, October 15, 2010.

Journal Times. "After Racine Man." January 9, 1899.

———. April 7, 1890.

———. "Biggest Buy in Town." December 24, 1961.

———. "Bohemian Society Has Celebration." March 9, 1914.

———. "Is Hurt in Saloon." September 30, 1911.

———. "Is It Here?" June 17, 1962.

———. July 18, 1892.

———. June 10, 1986.

———. "Lured from Home." June 2, 1891.

———. May 2, 1922.

———. May 9, 1986.

———. "Mrkvicka." July 15, 1892.

———. "Restaurant Men Buy Site Near Car Barnes." January 14, 1920.

———. "Richter Bldg. to Open Again as Restaurant." August 23, 1964.

———. "Richter Thinks Jack Will Win." May 21, 1921.

———. "Saturday Evening, Dec. 23." December 23, 1899.

McDowell, Jeremie, employee, Ivanhoe Pub & Eatery. In discussion with the author, September 3, 2021.

Nicholson, Doug, owner, Ivanhoe Pub & Eatery. In discussion with the author, July 15, 2021.

Preservation Racine Newsletter 2 (Summer 1996): 6.

Racine City Directory Collection. Racine Heritage Museum Archives, Racine, WI.

Racine Journal. "Attempted to Kill Himself." March 10, 1908.

———. "Ed. Schowalter Arrested; Bail of $100 Is Given." January 18, 1907.

———. "Mutilated Body Is Ghastly Clue to Lake Tragedy." May 14, 1912.

———. "Resort Is Raided." July 2, 1912.

Chapter 3

Dahlberg, Joyce. "Wigley Building Houses Racine's Past." *Journal Times*, March 12, 1978.

Donahue, Kelroy. "Street Scene: This Basement." *Journal Times*, April 5, 1983.

Givens, Billy, medium, Spiritually Charmed, in discussion with the author. November 21, 2022.

Jones, Stephanie. "The Haunted History of Downtown Racine." *Journal Times*, October 15, 2010. journaltimes.com/news/local/the-haunted-history-of-downtown-racine/article_db1dd216-d8e1-11df-b476-001cc4c03286.html.

Preservation Racine Newsletter (Summer 2001).

Racine Public Library. Downtown Racine Haunted Walking Tour Script. August 17, 2022.

Subject Index. Wigley Surname Cards. Racine Heritage Museum Archives, Racine, WI.

Part II

Daily Morning Advocate, December 19, 1853.

"DeKoven Center—Racine WI Real Haunt." Wisconsin Haunted Houses.com. www.wisconsinhauntedhouses.com/real-haunt/dekoven-center.html.

Fisk, Terry. "DeKoven Center." UnexplainedResearch.com. www.unexplained research.com/files_spectrology/dekoven.html.

Ghosts of America.com. www.ghostsofamerica.com/5/Wisconsin_Racine_ghost_ sightings14.html.

———. www.ghostsofamerica.com/5/Wisconsin_Racine_ghost_sightings18.html.

Helmick, Ron, founder, Racine Paranormal Investigators, and Michael Sorensen, medium, Racine Paranormal Investigators, in discussion with the author. January 26, 2023.

Journal Times. "Evergreen Burying Ground Dedicated Here in June 12, 1851." May 5, 1931.

———. "Little Known About Early Cemetery." July 14, 1984.

————. "A Mystery Unearthed." November 17, 2017.

Lardinois, Anna. "Winslow Elementary School: 1325 Park Avenue." In *Milwaukee Ghost and Legends*, 25–27. Charleston, SC: The History Press, 2018.

Racine Daily Journal. "Early Days." October 24, 1885.

————. November 12, 1886.

————. "Students Ghastly Find." February 13, 1902.

————. "That Skeleton." November 26, 1890.

————. "Vandals at Work." May 5, 1894.

Racine Journal. "Buried in Racine in 1846." May 5, 1905.

Racine Journal Times. "Bones Found in Wastewater Plant Sand." October 14, 1989.

————. "Historic Racine College, Episcopalians Shrine, Will Observe Centennial." February 28, 1952.

Racine Review. June 7, 1928.

————. "Old Cemetery to Figure in Court Battle." December 14, 1928.

Vertical Index. Folder 129.02 Winslow Elementary School. Racine Heritage Museum Archives, Racine, WI.

Chapter 4

Blausten, Elizabeth. "150th Anniversary of Masonry." *Journal Times*, October 27, 1998.

Colbert, Lucy. "A 'New' Masonic Temple Has Emerged from 'Old.'" *Racine Journal News Sunday Bulletin*, March 13, 1960.

Delvin, Sean. "Another Historic Home 'Victim' of Progress." *Journal Times*, March 24, 1967.

Helmick, Ron, founder, Racine Paranormal Investigators, and Michael Sorensen, medium, Racine Paranormal Investigators, in discussion with the author. January 26, 2023.

Kubik, Rachel. "That's the Spirit: Racine Paranormal Investigators Visit Social on Sixth, Seek More Haunted Locations." *Journal Times*, May 5, 2021.

Preservation Racine Newsletter no. 2 (Summer 1994): 2.

Shoreline Leader. "Dedication at Masonic Temple." May 11, 1978.

Spencer, Wendy, events coordinator, Masonic Center, in discussion with the author. September 8, 2021.

Tancill, Karen B. "Masonic Temple for Sale." *Journal Times*, May 4, 1988.

Vertical Index. Folder 656.02 Main Street: 1012 Main Street. Preservation Racine Tour of Historic Homes September 2004 booklet. Racine Heritage Museum Archives, Racine, WI.

Vertical Index. Folder 656.02 Main Street: 1012 Main Street. Preservation Racine Tour of Historic Homes Fall 2016 booklet. Racine Heritage Museum Archives, Racine, WI.

Vertical Index. Folder 656.02 Main Street: 1012 Main Street. Racine Heritage Museum Archives, Racine, WI.

Vertical Index. Folder 820 Durand. Racine Heritage Museum Archives, Racine, WI.

Vertical Index. Folder 840 Masons (Racine). Preservation Racine Tour of Historic Homes 1990 booklet. Racine Heritage Museum Archives, Racine, WI.

Chapter 5

Burke, Michael. "Hughes House: A Short History." *Journal Times*, April 16, 2006.

———. "Is the Hughes House B&B Haunted?" *Journal Times*, April 16, 2006.

———. "On the Lake." *Journal Times*, April 16, 2006.

Journal Times. "Old Haunts." October 31, 1998.

Larson, Jessica. E-mail correspondence with author. February 2023.

Obituary Index. Kearney File. Thomas M. Kearney Jr. Obituary, *Racine Journal-Times*, January 19, 1959. Racine Heritage Museum Archives, Racine, WI.

Russel James Larson obituary. *Journal Times*, July 30, 2002.

Scheck, Matt. E-mail correspondence with author. July 2021.

Schubring, Mike. E-mail correspondence with author. May 2021.

Vertical Index. Folder 820 Vance. Louis T. Vance obituary, October 10, 1952. Racine Heritage Museum Archives, Racine, WI.

Chapter 6

Butterfield, C.W. *History of Racine and Kenosha Counties 1879*. Chicago: Western Historical Company, 1879.

Case 11-00009 Bill & Bob's 10-22-2011. DVD. South East Wisconsin Paranormal Investigation Team. October 22, 2011.

Givens, Billy, medium, Spiritually Charmed, in discussion with the author. November 21, 2022.

Groth, Bob, and Bill Hansen, homeowners, Peck House, in discussion with the author. November 11, 2022.

Journal Times. "Hit by Auto, Thomas E. Sanders, Prominent as Educator, Dies." November 14, 1938.

———. "Peck." February 21, 1889.

Pfost, Marcia. "The Erastus C. Peck House." 2021 Preservation Racine Tour of Historic Homes Booklet.

Portrait and Biographical Album of Racine and Kenosha Counties. Chicago: Lake City Publishing Company, 1892.

Racine Journal. "Peck." February 27, 1889.

Subject Index. Peck Surname Cards. Racine Heritage Museum Archives, Racine, WI.

Urban Aesthetics Commission. *Racine Architectural Survey*. Ann Arbor, MI: Johnson, Johnson & Roy Inc., April 1974.

Vertical Index. Folder 840 Royal Arcanum. Racine Heritage Museum Archives, Racine, WI.

Chapter 7

Cuellar, Annette, homeowner, e-mail correspondence with author. May 2021–February 2023.

———, in discussion with the author. February 17, 2023.

Journal Times. "Dewey Mickelson." June 25, 1985.

———. "Eleanor L. Schaek." July 30, 2004.

———. "Otto Kruck." N.d.

———. "Report Finding Woman's Body." August 31, 1969.

Khrysten. "Racine, WI Residence." Paranormal Stories. paranormalstories. blogspot.com/2006/04/racine-wi-residence.html.

Chapter 8

Anonymous (Racine resident). Facebook comments, May 2021.

Fusko, Johanna, Racine resident, Facebook Messenger correspondence with author. January 2023.

Givens, Billy, medium, Spiritually Charmed, in discussion with the author. November 21, 2022.

Helmick, Ron, founder, Racine Paranormal Investigators, and Michael Sorensen, medium, Racine Paranormal Investigators, in discussion with the author. January 26, 2023.

Johnson, Bob. Notes on haunted Racine County locations. Folder 143 Haunted Houses/Ghosts. Racine Heritage Museum Archives, Racine, WI.

Journal Times. "County Institutions 'High Ridge Hospital.'" November 20, 1970.

———. "County of Racine Operates 5 Institutions; All Showed Progress during Past Year." January 7, 1939.

———. "County to Halt Farm Operation." March 12, 1959.

———. "Defense Rests in Overson Case; Arguments Scheduled March 31." March 20, 1942.

———. "Employees on Strike at County Institutions." August 31, 1971.

———. "Overson Free on 3 Counts, Fined on 4th; Wife Cleared." June 26, 1942.

———. "Racine Psychiatrist Criticizes Facilities at County Hospital." April 29, 1954.

————. "State Rests Case against Overson." March 13, 1942.

————. "Sunny Rest Annex, Recently Completed at Cost of $50,000, to Be Dedicated Soon." November 15, 1939.

————. "TB Loses Status as No. 1 Killer." April 5, 1964.

Matthews, John. "High Ridge Developer Restarts Construction." *Journal Times*, June 2, 1989.

Racine Journal. "Abandon Old Basis of Equalization." November 22, 1910.

————. "Insane Asylum Self Sustaining." November 22, 1910.

Racine Journal News. "Death Claims Man Who Gave His Life to a Hobby." May 12, 1915.

————. "More Care to Be Given to Graves of the Poor." November 21, 1916.

————. "Not to Remove Bodies." October 17, 1916.

Various Newspaper Articles. Folder 133.01 High Ridge Hospital. Racine Heritage Museum Archives, Racine, WI.

Chapter 9

Anonymous (teacher). Facebook Messenger correspondence with author. May–June 2018.

Case 180615 Evergreen Academy, Paranormal Investigators of Milwaukee, June 15, 2018.

Helmick, Ron, founder, Racine Paranormal Investigators, and Michael Sorensen, medium, Racine Paranormal Investigators, in discussion with the author. January 26, 2023.

Journal Times. "Compassion Built into Taylor Home by Racine Couple 100 Years Ago." November 24, 1968.

————. "Death Takes 'Miss Nellie' from Racine Orphan's Home Which She Entered as a Lame, Young Girl 60 Years Ago." March 29, 1933.

————. "Medora Roskilly Dies Suddenly." January 7, 1952.

————. "Taylor Home Adopts New Concept of Child Care." October 9, 1966.

————. "Taylor Memorial Monument Dedicated." November 15, 2017.

————. "Taylor Orphan Asylum." August 20, 2003.

Killackey, Brent. "Winslow Students Find a New Home at Johnson Elementary." *Journal Times*, October 18, 2005.

Racine Daily Journal. "The Suicide of Nora Harnett." April 29, 1899.

Vertical Index. Folder 133.04 Taylor Home. Racine Heritage Museum, Racine, WI.

Chapter 10

"AIR Investigation Report on Chances Restaurant February 20th, 2010." Anomaly Investigation Research, March 2010.

Burlington Free Press. January 22, 1913.

———. March 24, 1921.

Burlington Gazette. June 12, 1860.

———. "Union House." May 14, 1859.

Burlington Standard Press. "Building Still Standing after 120 Years of Continuous Use." April 12, 1956.

Chances Menu. Chances Food & Spirits, Rochester, WI.

Givens, Billy, medium, Spiritually Charmed, in discussion with the author. November 21, 2022.

Godfrey, Linda S., and Richard D. Hendricks. "Rochester," 240. In *Weird Wisconsin.* New York: Barnes & Noble Publishing, 2005.

"History of Chances Restaurant." Anomaly Investigation Research, March 2010.

Lacher, J.H.A. "Racine County." In *The Taverns and Stages of Early Wisconsin*, 141. Madison: State Historical Society of Wisconsin, 1915.

Norman, Michael. "Someone to Watch Over Me." In *Haunted Wisconsin*, 140–48. Madison: Terrace Books, 2011.

Schuerman, Tom, Sue Splan and Sarah Coots (owner, owner's sister and owner's daughter, Chances Pub & Eatery), in discussion with the author. April 10, 2022.

Standard Democrat. March 21, 1924.

———. October 19, 1923.

Chapter 11

Burlington Cemetery Association, Inc. "Home." www.burlingtoncemeterywi.com.

cjschmidt425. "Legend Tripping Episode 3: Burlington Public Cemetery." YouTube. June 19, 2008. Video, 9:16. www.youtube.com/watch?v=An89JnxF1uo.

Journal Times. "Burlington Cemetery Gets 15-Acre Addition." January 2, 1942.

———. "Help Sought with Cemetery Cleanup." May 15, 2003.

Kat Von J. "The Burlington Cemtery Incident (Legend Tripping) 6.14.2008." YouTube. June 18, 2008. Video, 5:24. www.youtube.com/watch?v=34vh3VsHcDg.

———. "Episode 2 of the Burlington Incident case no. B261908." YouTube. June 20, 2008. Video, 8:34. www.youtube.com/watch?v=9Di94Kf6NlU.

Milatz, Bill. "Burlington Cemetery Board Says Thanks." *Journal Times*, May 7, 2017.

MW Desperados. "Burlington Cemetery Final Chapter." YouTube. May 10, 2023. Video, 31:27. www.youtube.com/watch?v=qTCn-m61-Ew.

———. "Burlington Cemetery Part 1." YouTube. June 8, 2022. Video, 29:24. www.youtube.com/watch?v=NdU-cYru8gU.

———. "Burlington Cemetery Part 2." YouTube. June 15, 2022. Video, 34:04. www.youtube.com/watch?v=P5qy8LweJdw.

"National Register of Historic Places Registration Form." United States Department of Interior Services: NPS Form 10-900 for Burlington Cemetery Chapel. August 16, 2013.

Reed, Don. "Early Settlers of Burlington Buried on a Quiet Hill Near Browns Lake." *Journal Times*, June 19, 1955.

Shea, Mike, investigator, MW Desperados. E-mail correspondence with author. May 2023–June 2023.

Sutherland, Mary. "Chapter 1 Haunted Cemeteries." In *Haunted Burlington, Wisconsin*, 23–26. Charleston, SC: The History Press, 2014.

Williams, Scott. "Cemetery Buried in Financial Problems." *Journal Times*, February 9, 2023.

ABOUT THE AUTHOR

Working at the Racine Heritage Museum in high school, Rory Graves discovered a passion for local history and pursued a history and anthropology degree from the University of Wisconsin. After receiving their BA, Graves continued working in the museum industry, and a love of storytelling led them to sharing Racine's bizarre and often overlooked history on their website, the Unconventional Historian (www.unconventionalhistorian.com). In their free time, Rory Graves loves staying at home watching horror movies with their wife and two cats.

FREE eBOOK OFFER

Scan the QR code below, enter your e-mail address and get our original Haunted America compilation eBook delivered straight to your inbox for free.

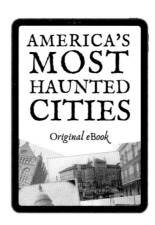

ABOUT THE BOOK

Every city, town, parish, community and school has their own paranormal history. Whether they are spirits caught in the Bardo, ancestors checking on their descendants, restless souls sending a message or simply spectral troublemakers, ghosts have been part of the human tradition from the beginning of time.

In this book, we feature a collection of stories from five of America's most haunted cities: Baltimore, Chicago, Galveston, New Orleans and Washington, D.C.

SCAN TO GET
AMERICA'S MOST HAUNTED CITIES

Having trouble scanning? Go to:
biz.arcadiapublishing.com/americas-most-haunted-cities